W9-CUH-583

A QUICK TRIP TO OBJECTLAND

A QUICK TRIP TO OBJECTLAND:
Object-Oriented Programming with Smalltalk/V®

Gene Korienek

ARTIFACT, Inc.
Siesta Key, Florida

Tom Wrensch

Wrensch & Associates
Boulder, Colorado

PTR Prentice-Hall
Englewood Cliffs, NJ 07632

Library of Congress Cataloging-in-Publication Data

Korienek, Gene.
  A quick trip to ObjectLand : object-oriented programming with
  Smalltalk/V / Gene Korienek, Tom Wrensch.
     p. cm.
  Includes bibliographical references and index.
  ISBN 0-13-012550-4 (pbk.)
     1. Object-oriented programming (Computer science) 2. Smalltalk
  (Computer program language)   I. Wrensch, Tom.   II. Title.
  QA76.64.K66   1993
  005.13'3--dc20   93-4105
                                                             CIP

Editorial/production supervision
  and interior design: *BooksCraft, Inc.*
Prepress buyer: *Mary Elizabeth McCartney*
Acquisition editor: *Greg Doench*
Cover design: *Jerry Votta*
Cover art: *Jinsei Chok/The Image Bank*

 © 1993 by PTR Prentice-Hall, Inc.
A Simon & Schuster Company
Englewood Cliffs, New Jersey 07632

Smalltalk/V is a registered trademark of Digitalk, Incorporated.
ComputerLand is a trademark of ComputerLand Corporation.

The first edition of the book was © 1991 by ARTIFACT, INC. Printed January of 1991.

The publisher offers discounts on this book when ordered
in bulk quantities. For more information contact:

> Corporate Sales Department
> PTR Prentice Hall
> 113 Sylvan Avenue
> Englewood Cliffs, New Jersey 07632
>
> Phone: 201-592-2863
> Fax: 201-592-2249

Printed in the United States of America
10 9 8 7 6 5 4 3 2 1

ISBN   0-13-363086-2

Prentice-Hall International (UK) Limited, *London*
Prentice-Hall of Australia Pty. Limited, *Sydney*
Prentice-Hall Canada Inc., *Toronto*
Prentice-Hall Hispanoamerica, S.A., *Mexico*
Prentice-Hall of India Private Limited, *New Delhi*
Prentice-Hall of Japan, Inc., *Tokyo*
Simon & Schuster Asia Pte., Ltd., *Singapore*
Editora Prentice-Hall do Brasil, Ltda., *Rio de Janeiro*

CONTENTS

PREFACE

A conventional programming language book is a combination reference book and code examples book—with some explanatory comments squeezed in. We considered following the conventional format, but that did not seem like much fun. Besides, Smalltalk/V is not a conventional language. So we wrote this book as a dialogue between two characters, the Objective Wizard and a human named Jim.

This book will show you how to solve problems in the object-oriented paradigm and then implement solutions using the object-oriented programming language Smalltalk/V. This book is not a reference book; it is more like a storybook with To Do Lists. So, read it as you would read a story. But while you read, you should have some version of Smalltalk/V running in a computer next to you.

The conversation between Jim and the Objective Wizard contains English sentences interspersed with Smalltalk/V code. You can easily recognize the Smalltalk code because it is always in monospace type, like `this`.

This book can be read in about ten sittings. You should complete the To Do Lists. The completed To Do code is not included in the book because we don't want you to look at our solutions when the work gets hard. We want you to work through the difficulties and reap the learning rewards. If you really want to see our solutions, then check the "About the Authors" section to find out how to get in touch with us.

After teaching Smalltalk/V classes for a few years, we figured out how people learn Smalltalk/V. We have found this approach an extremely effective path to understanding object-oriented concepts, as well as to learning how to solve problems by writing code in Smalltalk/V.

Once you have read this book you probably will not need it again. You will need a more advanced book. We suggest you continue your journey by checking the references listed in the back of this book. Or look for a future ObjectLand book!

Gene Korienek
August 1992
Siesta Key, Florida

ABOUT THE AUTHORS

Both authors reside in ObjectLand and can be contacted only by specific message sends. They live there because life is encapsulated there and it is OK to respond with `doesNotUnderstand`.

Gene Korienek lives on an island in southeast U.S. ObjectLand. He communicates to the real world by putting messages in bottles and tossing them into the outgoing tide. He lives with a large, four-legged virtuality named "Blacky." The message interface to the Blacky object is basically: `sit`, `stay`, `no`, `no`, `no`, and `heyGetBackHere`. Blacky also responds to the `wannaGoForAWalk` and `wantSomethingToEat` messages—but since they always return true, Gene has stopped sending them.

When not writing books, Gene teaches Smalltalk classes, writes Smalltalk code, and engages in a cornucopia of normal human activities. In a past instantiation he was referred to as a `SeniorResearchScientist` object existing in a `LargeCorporation` domain, and he still tends to behave as such. Sending the `currentResearch` message to the Gene object will answer a large string that can be parsed into smaller strings, including: cognitive modeling, intelligent interacting objects, and proactive human computer interfaces.

Tom Wrensch currently lives in the mountainous U.S. ObjectLand. Contacting Tom by normal channels is not easy, but he usually hangs out on AOL ("twrensch"). Tom lives with one human, two cats, and four computers. He says that living with four computers is no problem as long as you don't plug the Macs and PCs into the same circuit. Unfortunately the same can't be said of the cats.

When not writing books, designing software, or implementing strange new programs, Tom has been known to eat and sleep. His favorite pastime is playing "Rogue" and "Daleks" simultaneously. When asked why he spends so much time with computers, he just blinks and mumbles something about humans not having debuggers.

Tom also had a previous instantiation as a `ResearchScientist` object in a `LargeCorporation` domain, but he has long since recovered from his experiences there. Despite this he learned four valuable lessons: he hates getting up early, thinks writing research reports is a pain, believes researchers are severely underpaid, and he really hates getting up early.

ACKNOWLEDGMENTS

With any activity this size there are always people behind the scenes who often affect the project as much as the authors. Thanks to: Beverly Wrensch, Bill Bazan, Larry Brown, Guppy Ford, Guy Asbury, Bill Murphy, Fred Albert, Steve Pevnick, Steve Guastello, Raul Cuellar, John Lambi, Mario DeSario, Jack Arnold, and Mark Schwarz for their help and friendship. Thanks to Cami Ford for providing a mirror and to Dr. Botic for providing a personality.

0

AS OUR STORY BEGINS

Jim, a member of a software development group for a Fortune 100 corporation, joins two colleagues in the corporate coffee room. He loosens his tie, then rubs his eyes. His friends are discussing the difficulties inherent to their job: how software is expensive to develop, it's difficult to change, and it often doesn't work quite right and is error prone—despite the substantial investment of time it takes to create.

Jim nods sympathetically. He knows just what they mean. He's been puzzling through a development problem for days.

"Hey, fellas! Couldn't help but overhear!" A new member of the development team leans across a neighboring table. "But don't despair. It's a simple matter; all you need to know about are objects, messages, methods, inheritance, polymorphism, and encapsulation." He stands and pulls a brochure from his blazer pocket. He flips it to Jim and wiggles his eyebrows. "Just came back from there myself. Might be the answer to your problems."

Jim picks up the brochure as the new employee walks to the door. Just before leaving the room, he turns. "You'll see, fellas. The design process can be more intuitive. Complexity can be managed!!" Then he disappears into the corridor.

"Objects? Inheritance?" one of Jim's friends asks. "Do you know what that guy was talking about?"

Jim shrugs his shoulders. The other team members say good-bye, leaving him alone to page through the brochure, which recommends a revitalizing seminar for students and developers of software at a place called ObjectLand. According to the pamphlet, participants can enjoy high rates of code reuse through the design of general forms of specific solutions. . . . They can bask in the warmth of specialized forms of the solutions, benefiting from something called inheritance.

As Jim reads, his vision blurs. Exhausted from long hours at his desk, he sets the brochure aside and closes his eyes. "Boy, I'm tired," he thinks. "I sure could use a new perspective." Jim's world begins to spin, and his chin sinks to his chest. But immediately he awakens . . .

or so he believes. . . .

Jim   **Objective Wizard**

Hmgph, hmm, hey, where
am I?

> ObjectLand location.

Good morning?

```
Menu message:
  (Time now
      between: Midnight
      and: Noon)
  ifFalse: ['Not morning']
  ifTrue: ['Good morning']).
```

What?

Oh, excuse me. You must be a visitor to Object-
Land. I see from your label that you are a human
named Jim. I am the Objective Wizard.

In ObjectLand we say "good morning" by sending
the morning message to the greeting object:

```
Greeting morning.
```

The value returned from this message send is
determined by the greeting object, but a return is
guaranteed.

Why have you come to ObjectLand?

To find out about objects and
messages and such notions.

You have come to the right place, Jim. Everything
here in ObjectLand is an object. We objects can
respond only to messages sent to us, and our methods determine the response. Each of us has a set of

methods, one for each message we know how to respond to. Sometimes we inherit methods from our
parents, and sometimes they are part of our own
definitions. So, send me any message you want,
and I will execute one of my methods and return an
object to you.

Excuse me, there must be
some misunderstanding. I
come from a software development group in an important
company, and I need to learn
about software objects, messages, and methods. What
can you tell me about them?

Jim, ObjectLand is not real. It is a virtual place.
You are here in mind only, and only because you
have an interest in learning a new software paradigm. All objects here, including me, are virtual
(i.e., software objects). We objects view the world
through the messages sent to us. All I really know
about you is that you are an object sending me
messages that activate methods inside me. You are
now listening to my response to your last message.

As you know, objects exist in the physical world.
Your watch, for example, is a physical world object. Objects also can exist in your design world.
If your programming language supports objects,
then you can extend the existence of objects from
your design world into your implementation world.
Here in ObjectLand the programming language of
choice is Smalltalk/V. I am an object implemented
in Smalltalk/V.

Objects in Smalltalk/V are containers of information (variables), behavior (methods), and messages
(which activate the methods). In Smalltalk/V individual objects are not defined explicitly. Instead
you define classes of objects, and the individual
objects are instances of the class that characterizes
them.

Wait a minute, this sounds important. You seem to be describing objects by using the terms "object," "message," and "method." I just want to understand what an object is.

Please don't confuse me.

Jim, *object* refers to a conceptual entity that contains both state and behavior. In more conventional terms, it contains variables and code that can get and set the values of those variables.

Or you can think of an object as a package of information and descriptions of the manipulations of that information.

Jim, you can be thought of as an object. I know you contain some information or variables (that is, name, age, address, etc.), and I know you can exhibit behavior. For example, if I sent you the name message, you would behave by answering your name.

To think in object-oriented terms: you could be the receiving object of a message called "name"; when you receive the name message, you execute a chunk of code called a "method" (in this case your name method), resulting in behavior (that is, verbalizing your name).

Hey, this almost makes sense!

Of course it does. You are learning quickly. I accept you as my student. Congratulations.

How long will it take to learn enough to create some objects and take them back to my company?

Well, if you are willing to spend several hours a day, in a week you will be ready to begin implementing objects.

You mean it takes only a week to learn to program in Smalltalk?

No, it takes only a week or two to learn the object-oriented concepts, Smalltalk/V syntax, and programming environment. You also will learn how to learn Smalltalk/V. This last bit of knowledge will be the most valuable, for it will carry you the rest of the way.

Do you wish to be my student?

Yes. How do I start?

Send the turn message to the page.

1

OBJECTLAND

Contents at: 'Chapter 1'

Questions of Interest

What is an object?

What is a class?

What is an instance?

What is a message?

What is a method?

How do methods and messages relate?

What does Smalltalk code look like?

How do I read Smalltalk code?

Introduction

Welcome to ObjectLand!

Here begins your journey into the object-oriented paradigm. In this chapter you will learn the fundamental object-oriented concepts: object, message, and method. Because Smalltalk/V is a class-based implementation of an object-oriented language, you also will study the significance of class and instance and their roles in implementation.

The object-oriented paradigm and the Smalltalk language are significantly different from other programming languages and should be approached as something new. Avoid comparing what you already know about programming and what you are about to learn.

Goals for this Chapter

To understand and work with the following concepts:

Object

Class

Instance

Message

Method

In addition, we will show you how to read Smalltalk code. Reading code is the first step toward writing code.

When you finish this chapter, you will know about objects. More important you will have begun to think in terms of objects and messages. You will begin to see how the world consists of objects passing messages and executing methods.

Jim   **Objective Wizard**

Where am I?

> You are in ObjectLand, a virtual world that exists
> to simulate the real world. ObjectLand is made up
> of objects that communicate with one another by
> sending messages. We do things in ObjectLand by
> creating appropriate objects, telling them which
> messages they can respond to and how to respond
> to those messages.

Is that all?

> No, there is much more to ObjectLand, but it will
> take time to explain. Be patient.

What is an object?

> An *object* is an item in the real world. You are an
> object and so am I. Your pen, car, and TV are ob-
> jects. Objects also can be design entities in a soft-
> ware design document and implementation entities
> in an application, as you will see in later chapters.
>
> An *object* in Smalltalk is an implementation-level
> model of an object from the real or design world.
> A Smalltalk object is a conceptual entity with a
> private inside and a public outside. The inside con-
> tains information (sometimes called "state") in
> variables. This private inside can be accessed only
> by a message from the outside. Each object under-
> stands and responds to particular messages; each
> message activates a method, resulting in some
> behavior.

How about some examples of
objects?

> OK. Here is an example of a pen object:

A usable pen object must have a point or nib. It also must have a location, a direction, and something that stores its up or down state. It needs a drawing surface, of course, but that sounds like a different object.

In Smalltalk/V this pen object would be implemented as the Pen class, and the nib, location, direction, and up/down state would be stored as variables in the object. The variables also would contain objects. For example, the location would refer to a point on the drawing surface; the direction might be expressed as an integer number of degrees from direction 0 degrees. In both cases these are implemented as objects. Points are objects that store values for x and y coordinates. Integers also are objects.

Hmm, so an object is a thing that stores in variables the information it needs to do its job?

Yes!

Do objects really know things?

No, but you will find that we in ObjectLand always give objects more credit than they deserve for knowing what they do. We have found that by thinking in terms of intelligent objects we design more intelligent objects.

Think about it.

You used the term class?

The term object refers to the conceptual entity we have been talking about. In Smalltalk, however, objects with common characteristics are defined as a class, which simply means a group of similar objects.

How is a class used?

> The class contains the definition for the object. The information inside the object is described in the class definition. The class also has the ability to create an instance of itself when it receives the new message.

Instance? What's that?

> An *instance* is an object and is defined by its class definition. Most of the objects you will work with when implementing in Smalltalk will be instances of some class. You will occasionally work directly with a class.

Message? Could you explain that to me, please?

> Yes, a *message* is a request sent to an object, called the "receiver object," by another object, called the "sender object." The request always results in an action performed by the execution of a method. The set of messages to which an object will respond is called its "message interface" because an object's messages are its interface to other objects.

Method?

> A *method* is a piece of Smalltalk code. Every message, when received by an object, activates a method. Methods are associated with a particular class or instance.

Could you tell me again what an object is?

> Sure. An object contains information and descrip-

tions of how to manipulate that information. You can think of it as a combined chunk of data and procedure. Or you can think of it as a small computer with its own protected memory and its own set of procedures to act on the contents of its memory.

An object in Smalltalk is always either a class or an instance. In either case the object is defined by its class. The class definition consists of:

> class variable names
> instance variable names
> pool dictionaries
> class methods
> instance methods

How about an example of a class definition?

Sure!

The Pen object is a good example. First we implement it as a class called Pen. The Pen class definition would look like this:

class name:	Pen
instance variable names:	nib
	location
	direction
	downState
class variable names:	none
pool dictionaries:	none

The remainder of the class definition is a list of messages and associated methods to which the class and its instances will respond. This is two different lists, one for the class and one for the instances.

How can I create an instance of class Pen?

Easy, send the `new` message to the class `Pen`.
The Smalltalk code would look like this:

```
Pen new.
```

OK, let me see if I have this right. The fundamental programming unit of Smalltalk is the object, and the object contains information in class, instance, and those pool things.

Pool variables, but do not worry about them now.

Objects do programmed behavior when a message is sent to them. They subsequently execute the corresponding method code.

Technically speaking, yep.

What happens after the method code is executed?

An action of some sort may have occurred, based on what the method code was written to do, but an object is always returned to the sending expression.

Huh?

Every message send results in an object being returned to the expression that sent the message.

Huh?

The fundamental unit of Smalltalk code is an *expression*, which consists of one or more message sends to objects. Consider the following expression:

```
'Smalltalk is easy' size
```

What you just read is real Smalltalk code. It reads: send the `size` message to the string object `'Smalltalk is easy'`. This message send will return (answer) the integer object 17 because the `size` message sent to a string object will answer (return) an integer that is the number of characters in the string. We will test this in a few minutes, but let's try a slightly more complex expression:

```
'Smalltalk is easy' asSet size
```

This expression reads: send the `asSet` message to the string object `'Smalltalk is easy'` and then send the `size` message to the set object returned from the `asSet` message send. This expression will return the integer object 11 because the `asSet` message returns a set object (because sets cannot contain redundant elements). The size message is then sent to the returned set object and answers an integer that is the number of characters in the set.

Wow, I can almost understand that!

By the end of Chapter 2 that expression will be baby talk to you. (OOPS, I sent a Smalltalk joke message.)

OK, a message send always returns an object, and an expression is a chunk of code that is made of one or more message sends. A method is one or more expressions, right?

Yes. And every message send has a message and a receiver object. The object to which the message is sent is the *receiver object*, and the object that sends the message is the *sender object*.

For future reference, the receiver object is stored in the pseudo variable `self`. You can access `self` and use it in your code. I will discuss it in Chapter 2.

Give me another example, and this time talk in terms of class, instance, class variables, and instance variables.

OK.

Let's build a piece of paper for our pen to write on. A usable paper object must have a height, a width, and a location that describes where it is. It also must contain the information that is drawn on it.

(Note: In Smalltalk this paper object would probably be implemented in a more general form of drawing medium. In ObjectLand we usually seek out general solutions to problems, then specialize our general solution to fit a particular need. This approach helps us reuse the general portion of our solution in each specialization, saving time and promoting an incremental approach to development.)

Height and width could be integer objects; location could be a point object; and the drawn image could be represented as a separate object. All would be stored as instance variables in every instance of paper.

In this particular implementation of paper, there are no class or pool variables. It is common to create classes that use only instance variables.

A partial message interface to the paper object might have the following messages:

`new`	Create a piece of paper
`location`	Answer the location

`move: aLoc`	Change the location
`size`	Answer the size
`height`	Answer the height
`width`	Answer the width
`display`	Display the paper
`color`	Answer the color

I understand this to a degree, but I need to do the implementation myself to understand completely.

All right. Start your machine.

Use the Smalltalk/V manual that came with your software to help you get to where Smalltalk/V is running and you are looking at the system transcript window.

Take your time, I will wait. . . .

Now you are in the Smalltalk/V programming environment. You are looking at a user interface implemented in Smalltalk. The source code for it, including much or all of the windowing system, is available to you. We will look at it later. At this time it would be a good idea to read the Smalltalk/V tutorial chapters that discuss the user environment and the standard windows.

Take your time, I will wait. . . .

I've worked with Smalltalk/V some, and I have several questions.

That is what I am here for. Ask away.

I understand what's here, but I'm unsure about what I should do with what.

First of all I should point out that the Smalltalk/V system is embedded in a programming environment, which you use when you bring up Smalltalk/V. The programming environment consists of a group of tools, such as the class hierarchy browser and the system transcript, which you can use to do various programming tasks.

Most of the programming tools are window-based. A window is an object whose job is to display information and get feedback from users such as yourself. Windows almost always have one or more menus which let users pick the actions they want performed.

I think I get it.

You should not have any trouble, but it may take some time to feel comfortable. Just remember that windows show information, and menus are for choosing actions.

It will help if you spend some time every day playing with the environment. But do not play too loudly—the environment *is* ObjectLand, and you might wake me up.

I'll be careful not to disturb you, Wizard.

What now?

We will implement a piece of virtual paper. Follow me through the process step-by-step:

1. Open up a class hierarchy browser. This tool allows you to browse (look at) the existing classes in the system. The Smalltalk/V tutorial explains how to use this tool.

2. Point to and select the class named Object. It is at the top of the list of classes.

3. Select "add subclass" from the "class pop up"

menu if you are using Smalltalk/VDOS or
V286. If your system is Smalltalk/VMac,
VWindows, or VPM, select the "New Subclass"
or "Add Subclass" option from the "Classes"
pull down menu.

4. Name the subclass `Paper`. Class names always
    begin with a capital letter.

5. Select "subclass" or accept the defaults in the
    subclass dialogue box.

6. The class definition is now displayed in the
    pane below the list of classes. Insert the follow-
    ing instance variable names between the single
    quotes next to `instanceVariableNames`:

    ```
    height
    width
    location
    color
    contents
    ```

    There are no class or pool variables for the
    `Paper` class.

7. Select the "save" option and save the contents
    of the pane.

8. Select the "new method" option in the method
    pane and type in the message name over the
    "messagePattern" template. Write a comment
    that describes what this method will do. The
    comment should go between the double quotes.
    Select and cut the remaining text (| temporaries
    | statements) in the pane because, for the mo-
    ment, you will not write code in these methods.

9. Select the "save" option in the method pane.

Repeat this for each of the following messages (all
are instance messages except new, which is a class
message):

```
new         Create a piece of paper
location    Answer the location
```

`move: aLoc`	Change the location
`size`	Answer the size
`height`	Answer the height
`width`	Answer the width
`display`	Display the paper
`color`	Answer the color

The class hierarchy browser has a "class" and an "instance" button. Make sure the class button has been pressed before adding class methods and that the instance button has been pressed before adding instance methods.

Whew! That was not easy.

No, it was not easy, but you now know much of the Smalltalk programming process.

What now?

You are ready for the To Do List. When you are finished, we will meet again to discuss the syntax of the Smalltalk/V language.

It will be fun!

Summary

New Terms

Object	Class Variable
Message	Instance Variable
Method	Receiver Object
Class	Sender Object
Instance	Expression

What Did You Learn?

The basics of handling the Smalltalk/V environment from the Smalltalk/V manual.

The relationship between class and instance.

The relationship between message and method.

How to add a new class.

How to add instance variables to a class definition.

ObjectLand is a weird place.

Words of Wisdom

Message and method are often but erroneously used interchangeably. This is an understandable mistake, but one that can be confusing. Remember that a message is sent from the outside world to an object, and a method is something inside the object that is activated by a message.

Classes are classes and instances are instances, but objects are everything.

To Do List

Load your system, following the instructions in the Smalltalk/V tutorial.

Read the tutorial chapters that discuss the user environment.

You are a human computer interface designer in a large but trivial company. Your job is to evaluate the Smalltalk/V user interface, recommending changes, fixes, and enhancements. You feel, as do I, that the best way to understand the user interface is to use it and itemize all its capabilities. You decide to explore the user interface and write a report about the user interface in a workspace window.

Describe the general user interface strategy. Then expand your description of the user interface strategy by labeling and describing every menu item. Group them by window. Start with the system menu.

Your report should look like this:

      Window

           Menu Name

                    Menu Item   **Function**

                    Menu Item   **Function**

Using the disk browser, save the contents of your report in a disk file.

Do the following tasks in a new workspace, then evaluate each with a "show it" command.

    Send the `today` message to the `Date` class.

    Send the `now` message to the `Time` class.

    Send the `factorial` message to the number `11`.

Use the class hierarchy browser to add a new class called `Book`. It should have three instance variables: `title`, `author`, and `text`. It does not need any class or pool variables.

2

SMALLTALK/V: THE LANGUAGE

Contents at: 'Chapter 2'

Questions of Interest

How do I define a class?
How can I create an instance?
How do I write a method?

Introduction

In Chapter 1 you took a quick trip to ObjectLand, where you experienced how we think of objects as computational entities. And you learned a little about how to design software from objects and messages. Chapter 8 will discuss object-oriented thinking and design in much more detail. For the moment you will read more about the syntactical components of Smalltalk so we can begin to express object-oriented thoughts in terms of object-oriented implementations.

In Smalltalk a distinct separation exists between the language's capabilities, which are simple and compact, and the more extensive capabilities of the class hierarchy. The language, though, is the doorway into reading, understanding, and modifying the class hierarchy.

Goals for this Chapter

To understand:

1. the syntax of the language
2. the order of message execution
3. the scope and use of variables

To write Smalltalk code.

To learn the rules of the compiler.

When you are finished with this chapter you will have written a little Smalltalk code and will understand compile-time and run-time error messages.

Jim   **Objective Wizard**

Hey, Wiz! It's been a while.
Would you go over the basic
concepts for me?

Sure.

An object is a computational entity that contains
personal data in the form of variables and behavior
in the form of methods. There are two kinds of objects: class and instance. Every instance "belongs"
to exactly one class.

An instance object contains personal data in the
form of instance variables and behavior in the form
of instance methods. A class contains data in the
form of class variables and behavior in the form of
class methods. While an instance has its variables
all to itself, a class must share its variables with its
instances.

Pool variables work in much the same way as class
variables; they are defined at the class level and are
accessible by all of a class's instances. But they are
different in that several classes can access the same
set of pool variables at the same time. Pool variables are used for boring things such as storing
character constants, and we will not talk about
them very much.

Hey! What about messages?
Don't they belong in here
somewhere?

They certainly do. Messages are how objects com-
municate with one another. A message is sent
from one object, the sender object, to another, the
receiver object, where it activates a method. The
method executes, doing some work, and then returns an object to the sender.

That sounds a lot like a function call.

In some ways—but it is best to forget about such
comparisons. It will be easier if you learn this new
material without prior associations.

I'll try. I think I understand
all that stuff now. How about
the syntax?

Fine. First let us discuss the syntax associated with
objects because it is easy.

Class objects are referred to by class names. Class
names begin with a capital letter.

Instance objects do not have names but can be accessed in three ways:

1. the `self` pseudo variable
2. the returned object in an expression
3. a variable or argument

How is `self` accessed?

Remember, `self` is always the receiver object. To
be exact, `self` is the object that received the message that activated the method currently executing.
To access `self`, just treat it as if it were an argument to the method.

That's easy. What's next?

Messages and message syntax. Messages have
names called "message selectors." Some messages
have one or more arguments that they carry along
when they are sent to an object.

If some messages have arguments and others don't, how

does that change the syntax of
the message?

There are three message forms:

Message Form	Arguments
unary	none
binary	one
keyword	one or more

Tell me about unary mes-
sages.

Unary messages are messages with no arguments.
They are common in the existing system, and you,
as a designer/implementer, will add many more.
Unary messages always begin with a lowercase
letter.

What are unary messages
used for?

Use them whenever you want to send a message to
an object and do not need to carry an argument
along.

Please show me some exam-
ples.

Messages without objects have no meaning, so I
will send example messages to example objects:

Expression	Returned Object
'Smalltalk' size	9
Pen new	aPen
Bag new	Bag()
1234 even	true
Time now	08:18:32

Read the above code. In all cases the object is the first piece of the expression, and the message is the second. Type each expression into a workspace, then evaluate it with a "show it." A textual representation of the returned object will be displayed on the screen.

Tell me about binary messages.

Binary messages are messages with one-and-only-one argument and a special syntax consideration. A binary message selector consists of one or two special characters—characters other than digits or letters.

What are binary messages used for?

They are used primarily for arithmetic operations and comparison, but they can be used anywhere a programmer wants to use them.

Please give me some examples.

OK. I will use arithmetic examples in all cases but one. The one nonarithmetic example is the , (comma) message, which is used to concatenate objects.

Expression	Returned Object
3 + 4	7
61//20	3
10 < 20	true
'Small', 'talk'	'Smalltalk'
#(1 2), #(3 4)	(1 2 3 4)

Read the above code. In all cases the receiver object is the first piece of the expression, the message is the second, and the argument is the third. Type each expression into a workspace, then evaluate it with a "show it." A textual representation of the returned object will be shown on the screen.

Tell me about keyword messages.

Keyword messages are messages with one or more arguments. Keyword message selectors always start with a lowercase letter and are made up of pieces called *keywords*. Each keyword starts with a letter and ends with a : (colon). There is one keyword for each argument.

What are keyword messages used for?

They can be used for any message send requiring one or more arguments. With the exception of arithmetic and comparison, keyword messages normally are used when one or more arguments should be passed with the message send.

Please give me some examples.

No problem. Each of these expressions includes just one keyword message send:

Expression	Returned Object
| ```
Smalltalk
  at: #Pi
  put: 3.14.
``` | 3.14 |
| `Array new: 3.` | (nil nil nil) |
| ```
50
  between: 10
  and: 90.
``` | true |
| `Bag new add: 'Stuff'.` | 'Stuff' |

Read the above code. The receiver object is always the first piece of the expression, but the keywords of the message selector and the arguments alternate. Type each expression into a workspace, then evaluate it with a "show it." A textual representation of the returned object will be displayed on the screen.

Are there any other message forms?

No . . . well, there is one other, but it is not really a message form. It is more of a programmer's convenience. Called a *cascade message*, it is a way of connecting messages. By tacking on a ; (semicolon), you can send more than one message to the same receiver object.

Example without cascade:

```
MyPen := Display pen.
MyPen up.
MyPen black.
MyPen goto: 10@10.
MyPen direction: 360.
MyPen down.
MyPen go: 100.
```

Same example with cascade:

```
Display pen
    up;
    black;
    goto: 10@10;
    direction: 360;
    down;
    go: 100.
    yourself.
```

(If you are using Smalltalk/VDOS, V286 or VMac use Pen new instead of Display pen.)

In the first example you create an instance of class
Pen by sending the new message to the global
variable Display and assigning the instance that
is created to the global variable MyPen. You then
send messages to MyPen so it will do penlike
things. Note that you have to explicitly state the
object (MyPen). Note also that there is a . (period) at the end of each line. The period, the statement terminator, means each line is an individual
statement.

In the second example you accomplish the same
task with fewer words. The ; (semicolon) tells
Smalltalk to send the next message to the same
object that the previous message was sent to.

The message yourself is usually included as the
last message send in cascade messages because it
forces a return of the receiving object. The message yourself always returns self. This is
considered good programming style because it
guarantees control over what is returned from the
series of message sends.

I am a little confused by this
returned value stuff.

Every message send returns an object. With cascaded messages, the object returned is whatever
the last message send returns. When you include
the message yourself as the final message, you
ensure that the receiving object, self, will be
returned. Because cascade messages do multiple
operations to a single object, returning that object
is usually desired.

When do I use cascade messages?

Whenever you want to send several separate messages to the same object. It is used often in pen
drawing code.

What is a statement in Smalltalk?

> A *statement* is one or more message sends terminated by a period. The period is optional at the end of the last statement in a method.

Can a statement have more than one message send?

> Sure.

How about some examples of complex statements?

> Later. By the way, statement and expression mean the same thing in Smalltalk.

How does Smalltalk decide the order in which messages are executed?

> There are rules for the order of execution.

What are those rules?

> Expressions are executed in the following order:
>
> 1. code in parentheses
> 2. unary message sends (left to right)
> 3. binary message sends (left to right)
> 4. keyword message sends
> 5. assignments
> 6. returns

Show me an example.

```
Price := 87.0 + (12.00 * 3) +
         5000 / 50.
```

The above expression would be executed in this order:

Code	Returned Object
12.00 * 3	36.0
87.0 + 36.0	123.0
123.0 + 5000	5123.0
5123.0 / 50	102.46
Price := 102.46	102.46

Would you read this code for me?

Yes! I am happy you asked because code reading is one of the most important skills you can learn. In fact, you should try to read all Smalltalk code you see. I will give you an example of what Smalltalk code reading sounds like.

Send the binary message * to the instance of class Float 12.00 with the instance of class Integer 3 as an argument. Return the instance of class Float 36.0.

Send the binary message + to the instance of class Float 87.0 with the instance of class Float created by the last message send as the argument. Return the instance of class Float 123.0.

Send the binary message + to the instance of class Float 123.0 with the instance of class Integer 5000 as the argument. Return the instance of class Float 5123.0.

Send the binary message / to the instance of class Float returned from the last message send with the instance of class Integer 50 as the argument. Return the instance of class Float 102.46.

Finally, assign the instance of class `Float`
`102.46` to the global variable `Price`. `Price` is
now `102.46`, which is an instance of class
`Float`.

Would you do that again with
some different code?

Yes. Consider the following:

```
#(1 2 3 3 45 43 43 99 10 12 3 7)
    asSet
        asSortedCollection
            asArray.
```

This code sends the unary message `asSet` to the
instance of `Array` `#(1 2 3 3 45 43 43 99
10 12 3 7)`, which answers an object that is an
instance of the class `Set`. The `asSortedCol-
lection` message then is sent to the instance of
class `Set`, which was answered from the `asSet`
message send. The `asSortedCollection`
message answers an instance of the class `Sorted-
Collection`, and the `asArray` message is sent
to that instance. The `asArray` message answers
an instance of the class `Array`.

This expression strips redundant elements from the
original array and answers a new array with the elements in ascending order.

How about doing it one more
time with different code?

Sure. Consider the following:

```
9 factorial
    between: (10 * 10000)
    and: (50 * 10000).
```

The unary message `factorial` is sent to the integer instance `9`, returning the integer instance
`362880`. The `between:and:` keyword message

then is sent to `362880` with the arguments (`10` `*` `10000`) and (`50` `*` `10000`). Since the arguments are in parentheses, they are evaluated before the keyword message. These evaluations return integer instances of `100000` and `500000`, respectively. The `between:and:` is evaluated, determining that `362880` is between `100000` and `500000`.

The overall expression returns `true`.

How can you tell what is a class, instance, message, or variable?

Everything you read in a Smalltalk expression will be one of the following:

> class name
> constant object (number, string, etc.)
> message selector
> variable containing an object
> punctuation (^, :=, ; , " , # , ., etc.)

Every word you read in an expression is one of these five constructs.

If a word begins with a capital letter, then it is one of the following:

> class name
> global variable referencing an object
> class variable
> pool variable

If it is a class name, then look in the class hierarchy browser to find out more about it. If it is a global variable, then you can send an `inspect` message to it.

If a word begins with a lowercase letter, then it is one of the following:

local variable referencing an object
argument referencing an object
instance variable referencing an object
message

If it is a local variable or argument, it will be
declared somewhere in the method code. If it is an
instance variable, it will be part of the object's class
definition (you can look at the definition using the
class hierarchy browser). If it is none of the above,
it is a message.

**What global variables are
available?**

There are many global variables already in the
Smalltalk system. You can examine all the global
variables by using this piece of code:

```
(Smalltalk reject: [:value |
        value isKindOf:
Behavior])
        inspect.
```

The easiest way to add a new variable is to use it.
The system will ask if you want to make the new
variable a global variable; answer "yes" and you
are set. You can also add new global variables by
using this piece of code:

```
Smalltalk at: #MyVariable put: nil.
```

The Smalltalk in both pieces of code refers to
an object that keeps track of all of the global variables. If you want to see all the global variables,
including the class names, type:

```
Smalltalk inspect.
```

**What does the syntax of the
language look like?**

There is a summary of the Smalltalk syntax at the

end of this chapter. Look it over; study it a bit. But the best way to learn syntax is to use it.

Do any objects use a special syntax?

Yes, instances of `Array`, `Character`, `String`, and `Symbol` use special syntax. Another kind of object, called a block, also has a special syntax. Let us examine them one at a time.

Array—An array can be created by using a # (hash mark) followed by an ((open parenthesis) followed by some number of elements. The array's end is marked with a) (close parenthesis). Arrays built in this way can contain only strings, symbols, characters, and other arrays. Some examples:

```
#(1 2 47.9)
#($a 'Hi There')
#(ABC ($a $b $c))
```

The last array contains two elements: a symbol and an array. Note that the # (hash mark) is skipped when used inside the array.

Character—A single character object can be referenced by preceding it with a dollar sign. For example $a is the lowercase letter a, $3 is the character 3, and $$ is the character $.

String—Any sequence of characters enclosed in single quotes is a Smalltalk string. For example:

```
'Hello there'
'1 2 3 4'
'Smalltalk inspect'
```

Symbol—A symbol is a sequence of characters, just like a string—except when two symbols are created with the same sequence of characters, then they are always the same object. (This special property is not one you need to worry about now, but it is important for the way several parts of the Smalltalk system work.) Symbols are normally a single line with no spaces, starting with a letter, and they are preceded by a # (hash mark). Some examples:

```
#A
#between:and:
#name
```

Block—A block is a chunk of code packaged as an object. The syntax for a block is simply square brackets around some code. Other kinds of blocks have one or two arguments before the code, preceded by a : (colon) and followed by an | (upright line). Some examples:

```
[Terminal bell]
[:number | 10 * number - 1]
[:a :b | a raisedTo: b]
```

What about variables?

Variables refer to objects. If you are a variable, your issues of interest are:

1. duration of existence
2. scope of influence
3. capitalization
4. value (always an object)

What about their scope and usage?

Instance, class, and pool variables are included in the class definition. Local variables (including arguments) are defined within each method. Global variables are defined for the entire system.

Although added to the class definition, each instance has its own set of *instance variables*.

The values assigned to the instance variables differentiate instances of the same class. Instance variables for an object can be accessed only by methods activated by sending that object a message.

Class variables are used to describe information associated with an entire class. The class and all its instances have access to a class variable.

Global variables are available anywhere in the environment. They exist until they are explicitly removed. To add a new global variable:

```
Smalltalk at: #MyGlobal put: nil.
```

To remove one:

```
Smalltalk removeKey: #MyGlobal.
```

Pool variables are grouped into pool dictionaries. A class definition can access a pool of variables by adding the pool dictionary name to its class definition. Pool variables normally are used only to ease reference to constant values.

Local variables are available only in the method in which they are declared. The local variable, created when a method starts executing, exists until the method returns. Local variables include method arguments and block arguments. Treat block arguments as valid only between the square brackets defining the block.

Global, class, and pool variables always start with a capital letter. Instance and local variables begin with a lowercase letter.

Is that all?

No, there are also five *pseudo variables*: `nil`, `true`, `false`, `self`, and `super`. Pseudo variables are different: they cannot be assigned.

And in the cases of nil, true, and false, their values are always the same.

The pseudo variables nil, true, and false are instances of the following classes:

Class	Instance
UndefinedObject	nil
True	true
False	false

The pseudo variable self always refers to the receiver object. The pseudo variable super refers to the receiver object, but when a message is sent to it, it looks for the method in its superclasses method list. This improves code reusability when using inheritance, which I will discuss later.

I'm pretty sure I understand the different kinds of variables, but how do I set their value?

Oh, pardon me. The assignment is done using the : = (colon-equal) operator. Although it looks like a binary message send, it is actually a special operation. You may recall that in the order of execution an assignment was almost at the end of the list. Here are some examples of assignment:

```
Birthday := '2 Jan 1983' asDate.
total := x + y + z.
count := count + 1.
aString := 'I am a Smalltalk
basher'.
```

I should also mention the return operation, a ^ (caret) preceding an expression, answers the value to return from the method.

Since every message returns
some object as its value, then
must every method have a return operation in it?

Not exactly. If you do not put a return operation in
a method, the default is to return the receiver
object.

Now that I think about it, I
don't know how to write a
method yet.

It is not difficult. Let us look at a method and
discuss its structure:

```
raisedToInteger: anInteger
    "Answer myself raised to the
    integer power anInteger."
| answer |
answer := 1.
anInteger timesRepeat: [
    answer := answer * self].
^answer.
```

The first line in this method is the message pattern.
It includes the method's name (raisedToInte-
ger:) and declares the argument (anInteger).
The second and third lines are a comment. You
can place a comment almost anywhere within the
method code, but a comment just below the message pattern is standard. In the fourth line is
a local variable declaration for a variable called
answer. If you do not use any local variables,
you can eliminate the upright lines.

The last four lines contain the actual Smalltalk
code. We do not need to talk about what the code
does, but I should point out that the first line of
code is an assignment and the last line returns a
value from the method.

Why does the comment use myself as if it were a person?

In this case, myself here refers to the receiver object. It is common to write method comments in this manner because it gives the writer an easy way to refer to the receiver object. Writing comments in an anthropomorphic fashion also helps you think in terms of intelligent objects.

What happens if I make a mistake when adding a method?

When you try to save your new or modified method, the compiler will let you know if it does not like something. It will insert an error message just before the code the compiler thinks is wrong.

I think I understand, but what does some other code look like, how do I write it, and where does it go? Turn me loose, Wizard. I wanna write some Smalltalk code.

So I see! I suggest you go to the To Do List.

Summary

New Terms

Unary Message	Pool Variable
Binary Message	Pool Dictionary
Keyword Message	Global Variable
Cascade Message	Local Variable
Statement	Message Pattern

What Did You Learn?

The three message types and cascaded messages.

The order of execution.

How to read Smalltalk code.

The special syntax of arrays, characters, strings, symbols, and blocks.

Pseudo variables `true`, `false`, `nil`, `self`, and `super`.

How a method is put together.

Words of Wisdom

Take some time to learn how to use the "implementers" and "senders" options on the methods menu in the class hierarchy browser. They allow you to trace quickly who sends a message and what it is for.

When you see Smalltalk code, look at it. Read it to yourself, try to understand what it does. This will improve your comprehension of the system and Smalltalk programming techniques. Warning: Don't read the code out loud. People might think you're strange.

Watch your order of execution, particularly when doing numeric expressions. When in doubt, use parentheses.

Syntax Summary

Special Symbols

Symbol	Meaning	Example
: =	assignment operator	`pages := pages + 1.`
.	statement terminator	`A := A reversed.`
;	cascade protocol	
^	return the following object	`^name`
[ ]	block delimiter	`[Terminal bell]`
( )	expression delimiter	`salary := 3.47 * (43 + 5)`
:	keyword message	`Contents at: 'Chapter 1'`
" "	comment	`"This is a comment"`
' '	string	`'This is a string'`
#	symbol or array constant	`#(one 33 house xyz)`
$	character constant	`$ k`
|	local variables	`| anArray index |`

Scope of Variables

Variable	Scope
local	single method execution
instance	single instance
class	class and all its instances
pool	all classes that specify the pool dictionary
global	everywhere

Order of Execution

code in parentheses

unary message sends (left to right)

binary message sends (left to right)

keyword message sends
assignments
returns

To Do List

Your best friend owns a music store, and you have decided to help him implement a sales tracking system. Use the class hierarchy browser to add two new classes: CompactDisc and CDTrack .

CompactDisc should have three instance variables: title, artist, and tracks. CDTrack should have three instance variables: title, trackNumber, and length.

You have another friend who owns a computer store, and you have decided to help him too. Create a class to represent a diskette. Call it Diskette. Some of the characteristics you may want to represent are:

Instance Variable	Comment
type	DS, SS, HD, etc.
size	Diameter of disk
capacity	How much storage disk has
label	Name of disk
location	Which box in closet
lastUsedDate	Last time disk was used

Instance Method	Comment
location	Answer location of disk
location:	Set location to a new location
type	Answer type of disk
size	Answer size of disk
capacity	Answer capacity of disk
label	Answer name of disk
label:	Change name of disk
lastUsed	Answer last used date
lastUsed:	Update last used date

3

BACK TO OBJECTLAND

Contents at: 'Chapter 3'

```
#(
encapsulation
      get method
      set method
polymorphism
inheritance
      class-subclass hierarchy
      overriding inheritance
super)
```

Questions of Interest

When and what do I subclass?
How can I benefit from inheritance?

Introduction

In Chapter 1 you were introduced to the object-oriented programming paradigm, learning how objects are computational entitites in ObjectLand. You also saw how to design software from objects and messages. Chapter 8 will discuss object-oriented thinking and design in much more detail. In this chapter you will learn about three concepts: encapsulation, polymorphism, and inheritance. You also will read more about the class hierarchy.

Goals for this Chapter

To understand how to use encapsulation, polymorphism, and inheritance in design and implementation.

To map some small problems into object-oriented representations.

To learn more about the object-oriented paradigm.

Jim   **Objective Wizard**

Well, I'm back!

> Good! Let us get to work. I would like to introduce you to some of ObjectLand's moral fiber, especially three underlying capabilities that are particularly interesting: encapsulation, polymorphism, and inheritance.
>
> Let us look at them one at a time.

I'm game. What is encapsulation?

> *Encapsulation* describes the privacy of an object.

How can I use it?

> You do not have a choice; it is enforced. Objects are encapsulated by nature, but you can design objects whose role is to encapsulate. I will discuss these objects, called "encapsulators," in more detail in Chapter 9.

There's no way I can avoid encapsulation?

> No, but you can choose either to use it or to work around it. Encapsulation is not enforced to make your life difficult; it is a way to keep an object's inside from getting unexpectedly and incorrectly altered.

I think I see. Encapsulation keeps an object from getting trashed by some other object.

> Well put. And by knowing about encapsulation, you can write better code.

I don't quite see how encapsulation functions. If the object is private, how can I work with it?

An object can be accessed only by sending it a message. If an object's message interface does not include a way to access an instance variable directly, then you cannot look at or change that variable from outside.

So if I need to access information that's kept in an instance variable, I write methods that do it.

Yes! Very good, Jim. These messages are so common, they have names. A *get* method just gets and answers the value of an instance variable. A *set* method just sets the value of an instance variable.

I see. And what is polymorphism?

Polymorphism refers literally to the ability to assume different forms. In Smalltalk, *polymorphism* refers to a message's ability to assume different functions, depending on the receiving object.

How can a message behave differently, depending on the object it's sent to?

The message is a selector, while the method is the actual code that results in behavior. Polymorphism relies on this difference between message and method and the fact that Smalltalk uses dynamic, or late, binding of message to method. In Smalltalk the binding of a message to the method it will activate occurs when the message is sent. The method to be activated is picked based on the receiver object. So it is really the receiving object that determines what method is executed and, consequently, what function is performed.

How about some examples?

Sure! Look at the following code:

Expression	Answer
`3 + 4`	7
`3.2 + 3.14`	6.34
`(10 @ 30) + (10 @ 10)`	20 @ 40
`(1/2) + (32/64)`	1

Here the message + is sent to instances of four different classes: `Integer`, `Float`, `Point`, and `Fraction`. In each case the method activated answers the sum of the receiver and the argument; each summation, however, is done in a different way.

For example, while the sum of two integers is a primitive operation with no further Smalltalk code, the sum of two points looks like:

```
+ aPoint
     "Answer the sum of myself
     and aPoint."
  ^Point new
     x: (self x + aPoint x);
     y: (self y + aPoint y);
     yourself.
```

So the + message is polymorphic because it is part of the message interface for several classes, and each class implements it in the way that is most appropriate for it.

Different object-oriented languages have slightly different implementations of polymorphism, some of which are limited. Smalltalk's polymorphism works all the time for every message send.

How about some more examples?

Sure! Look at the following code:

Expression	Answer
`'ObjectLand' size.`	10
`#(q w e r t y ) size.`	6
`('one', 'two') size.`	6
`Set new`	
`    addAll: 'one', 'two';`	
`    size.`	5

Here the `size` message is sent to instances of class `String`, `Array`, and `Set`. Each answers the number of elements it contains, but each computes its number of elements differently.

In all these cases `size` answers the number of elements in the receiving object, though the method computing the size was different. Two objects receiving the same message should behave in a similar way.

How can I use polymorphism in my code?

First you need to learn which messages are used polymorphically in the class hierarchy. This simply takes experience, but you can augment your learning by selecting a message in a class hierarchy browser and then using the "implementors" option in the methods menu. The implementors window will open on a list of all classes that implement the message you chose. If there is only one item listed, then the message you chose is not used by more than one class and so cannot take advantage of polymorphism.

Second, begin to design using polymorphism. The robot exercises in this chapter's To Do List are good examples for designing with polymorphism.

I do not want to tell you more about this task because it is intended to be a problem-solving exercise for you.

What is the best way to learn more about polymorphism?

Design your projects to use polymorphism. It is particularly effective when used with inheritance.

Inheritance?

Inheritance is a conceptually simple but powerful problem-solving tool available to Smalltalk programmers. All Smalltalk classes exist in a class-subclass hierarchy. When you view the class hierarchy using a class hierarchy browser, you will notice that some classes in the class list are indented. An indented class is a subclass of the class it is indented from. Look at the following example:

```
Number
    Float
    Fraction
    Integer
```

In this example the class Number is the superclass of Float, Fraction, and Integer. Float, Fraction, and Integer are subclasses of Number.

So how is this class-subclass relationship useful?

Think of inheritance as a problem-solving tool rather than a concept. If you think of it as a concept, then it becomes something you must learn. If you think of it as a problem-solving tool, then it becomes something you can use. Do you see the distinction?

Yes, but I still don't know
what's useful about it.

In problem solving it is often useful first to solve a
piece of the problem in a general sense; then you
can solve that piece in a more specific way based
on the general solution.

With inheritance you can solve the general characteristics of the problem in a superclass, and
then create subclasses to implement the specific
solutions. The Number classes are a good example of this approach. (Class Number is a very
general solution to the problem of what it means
to be a number.) Much of the number behavior is
implemented in the Number class, but the subclasses implement specialized versions of numbers (that is, Integer, Float, Fraction). By
using inheritance, the subclasses inherit all the
variables and methods implemented in the Number class, and then proceed to add their own
variables and methods, becoming specializations
of Number.

Wow, and I am reusing much
of the code I write in the
Number class in the sub-
classes, right?

Right!

Just what is inherited?

All the methods and variables of a superclass are
available to its subclasses.

How about an example?

Explore the Number hierarchy and find out which
methods used in Integer and Float operations are actually inherited from Number or its su-

perclass `Magnitude`. Also, look for the methods from Number that have been overridden in `Float` and `Integer`.

Overriding inheritance?

Yes. When working with a subclass, you will realize at times that you are inheriting something you do not want. If you are inheriting variables of no use to your subclass, you can simply ignore them. If this happens often, or if there are many variables you do not wish to inherit, then redesign the superclass-subclass relationship and rebuild the classes. If you are inheriting methods you wish to use in a different manner in your subclass, then override them by implementing a method with the same message selector in the subclass.

If you wish to call an overridden method, use the `super` pseudo variable—the superclass version of the method will be used. Place `super` in your code before the message selector you are sending.

I don't understand that part about using `super` to call overridden methods. Could you explain it to me again?

Of course. The pseudo variable `super` works just like `self`, except it looks only for methods you inherit. By skipping your class's personal methods, it can call a method that has been overridden. This is the only reason `super` exists.

You will rarely use `super` except within the method that is overriding what you are trying to call. For example, the following method uses the overridden method to do most of its work:

```
initialize
        "Private - Initialize my
         instance variables."
super initialize.
z := 0.
```

This method first calls the method it is overriding, and then it initializes an extra instance variable.

How about an example of inheritance?

All right, but I want you to do some of the work. Pick an object for us to work with.

How about a book?

Fine. We can think about a librarian trying to keep track of a library's books. What things about a book would a librarian want to keep track of?

Let's see . . . title and author, and probably that number used to reference books.

The Dewey Decimal classification. I would like to add the number of pages as well.

Here is our definition so far:

```
Book (Subclass of Object)
    title
    author
    deweyNumber
    pageCount
```

What is our next step?

Hmm . . . earlier you said something about creating general solutions. Is this a good time to do that?

A very good time. Because a library is our intended audience, I think a general class called Document would be in order.

Sure, libraries have lots of

inventory besides books: magazines, reports, tapes. . . .

Good! For this example let us say that a Document has a title and deweyNumber. Now our design looks like:

```
Document (Subclass of Object)
    title
    deweyNumber

Book (Subclass of Document)
    author
    pageCount
```

Note that I included the superclass in parentheses after the class name. You will find such references very important when you start designing.

I believe I understand inheritance now, but it would help if you ran through all the concepts one more time.

Encapsulation protects the instance variables of an object from access by the outside world. Objects can be accessed only through their message interface. This saves you from worrying about some foreign code altering your object's instance variables.

Polymorphism is the ability of different objects to react differently to the same message. This property will help you when designing or writing code.

Inheritance is a programming tool that lets you implement general solutions to a problem in a class, and then specialize that solution by creating subclasses. Inheritance applies to both variables and methods, but only methods can be overridden.

Wow, these are some really new ideas!

Yes, and I suggest you learn them as "really new ideas." Do not try to fit them into your existing idea framework. If you want to use a truly object-oriented programming language, you must work with these ideas, which are very much the essence of the paradigm. Do not think of polymorphism as like "operator overloading" or methods like "procedures." Open up a new space in your imagination and learn something completely new.

Do not throw away your old paradigm—just learn to live with two paradigms. You will benefit from both.

I still am not sure what it means to program in Smalltalk.

That is because I have not asked you to program in Smalltalk. You have written Smalltalk code and created some classes, but you have not experienced the full programming process.

But you will in the next chapter. Good luck!

Summary

New Terms

encapsulation
polymorphism
inheritance
overriding inheritance

What Did You Learn?

What encapsulation is and what it means to you as a programmer.
What polymorphism is and how to find occurrences of it in the class hierarchy.
What inheritance is and how to identify it in the class hierarchy.
What is inherited.
How to override methods.

Words of Wisdom

Create your subclasses so they make sense. If you can't say with confidence that your subclass is a kind of its superclass, don't use it.

Good inheritance trees are bushy. It is easy to go too far when making subclasses.

Good inheritance schemes rarely go more than four or five classes down from class `Object`.

To Do List

You are a researcher at the Captain Video Memorial Robotics Lab; your task is to model the behavior of three robot designs. Each design uses a significantly different locomotive strategy.

`Robot 1`   is a humanlike critter that walks on two legs. It changes direction by activating a shape memory alloy muscle. It changes velocity by changing the step rate of its gait.

Robot 2   is a monopod that hops about on one leg and changes direction by pointing its leg to a different spot when it prepares for landing. It changes velocity by changing its landing angle.

Robot 3   is an amorphous creature that uses a pseudopodic mechanism for loco-motion. It changes direction by pumping a fluid into a segment of its pseudopod. It changes velocity by changing the fluid volume in the leading portion of the pseudopod.

Implement each robot design in terms of class definitions and message interfaces. You don't have to implement the method code, but you do have to write a comment to describe what each method will do after it is implemented.

When designing your class hierarchy, think of how you can use inheritance to in-crease code reusability.

When designing your message interfaces, think about behavior. Use polymorphism to facilitate extensibility.

4

NUMBERS ET AL.

Contents at: 'Chapter 4'

Questions of Interest

What are the arithmetic capabilities of Smalltalk?
What is the order of execution?
What about mixed-mode arithmetic?

Introduction

Numerical manipulation is a very common programming task. Many computer programming languages were created solely to ease large amounts of "number crunching." While Smalltalk is not one of those languages, it has very sophisticated numeric manipulation capabilities.

In Smalltalk numbers are represented as objects, and arithmetic is done by sending messages. This greatly influences how numbers are handled. In Smalltalk the behavior of numbers is defined within a higher level of abstraction found in the class `Magnitude`. By learning about numbers, you will learn how to deal with some of the other subclasses of `Magnitude`, such as `Date`, `Time`, and `Character`.

The `Number` class itself is an abstraction; actual numbers are represented by instances of subclasses of `Number`, such as `Float`, `Fraction`, and `Integer`.

Goals for this Chapter

To implement mathematical expressions in Smalltalk.

To see how the underlying characteristics and order of execution shape the behavior of Smalltalk's numerical capabilities.

To understand the capabilities and limitations of Smalltalk's current numeric manipulation system.

Jim   **Objective Wizard**

Hi, I'm back!

> I am busy right now. Could you come back later?

Well, I've come a long way.

> All right, all right. What do you want to know?

How about numbers? I need to do some arithmetic, and I'm not sure how to do it in Smalltalk.

> How serendipitous! I happen to be working in the `Magnitude` class hierarchy at this very nanomoment. I am considering extending some of its capabilities.

Oh . . . but I want to know about numbers, not magnitudes.

> I understand, Jim. Remember that in Smalltalk all objects are defined in classes and all classes reside somewhere in the class hierarchy. Remember also that classes inherit variables and methods from their superclasses, and they pass variables and methods on to their subclasses.
>
> Take a look at the `Magnitude` hierarchy. `Float`, `Fraction`, and `Integer` are subclasses of `Number`, which in turn is a subclass of `Magnitude`. Also notice that there are other subclasses of `Magnitude`.

```
Magnitude
  Association
  Character
```

```
Date
Number
    Float
    Fraction
    Integer
Time
```

All the specific number classes (`Float`, `Integer`, and `Fraction`) are subclasses of class `Number`.

The reasons for this arrangement are best understood by discussing this hierarchy's inheritance architecture. Let us start with the superclass of this hierarchy, class `Magnitude`.

Class `Magnitude` is an abstract class implemented to handle the comparing, ordering, and interval testing of instances of its subclasses. If you are interested in answers to questions such as

Is `324` less than `-123`?

Is `43` between `17` and `33`?

Is `Aug 4, 1991` later than `Jun 2, 1991`?

Is `2:17` later than `1:24`?

Does `M` come after `K`?

then class `Magnitude` provides the protocol for instances of its subclasses to make these kinds of comparisons. As an abstract class, `Magnitude` is intended to contain capability and protocol, not to be instantiated. In this case the subclasses of `Magnitude` must implement many of the capabilities described in `Magnitude`.

So `Magnitude` has the protocol for comparing instances of its subclasses. What about the subclasses?

The immediate subclasses are:

```
Association
```

```
Character
Date
Number
Time
```

I enjoy talking about all the classes in ObjectLand. But for reasons of brevity, after I outline the capabilities of each class, I will focus on only `Number` and its subclasses.

Class `Association` associates two objects in a particular direction. Heavily used by the `Dictionary` classes, it is rarely used directly. In fact, you need not be concerned with `Association`.

Characters in Smalltalk are represented as instances of the class `Character`. Its instances represent characters from the extended ASCII set from ASCII value 0 to 255.

Class `Date` is used to represent dates and includes methods to query and manipulate the date. I suggest you look at the method list for `Date`. Start by looking at the `today` class method.

Class `Time` is used to represent the time of day and includes methods to query and manipulate the time. I suggest you look at the method list for `Time`. Start by looking at the `now` class method.

Class `Number` is an abstract class that establishes the general behavior of "numberness." Class `Number` is never used directly, but it provides, through inheritance, the general structure for all numbers in the system.

Very interesting, but I have particular tasks that I need to do using numbers. I want to make sure Smalltalk can handle my needs. If I asked you some specific questions, would you answer them?

Ingrate! Have I not answered all your questions up to this point?

Yes, Wizard, but I want very specific answers this time because arithmetic is important in my application.

Very well, I will answer your questions in the most specific form I know—Smalltalk code. In return I want you to read each expression carefully, in the manner I taught you during our second meeting. I also will show you what is returned from each expression.

Will that be adequate?

Wonderful.

(3 + 4) x 22

Code	Returned Value
3 + 4 * 22	154

What? You got the correct answer, but the code looks like it should return 91.

You are reading it as if it was an arithmetic expression and computed along the conventional rules for evaluating arithmetic expressions.

Let me read it as a Smalltalk expression for you:

Send the + message to the integer object 3   with the integer object 4 as an argument. This message send returns the integer object 7, to which the message *   with the integer object 22 is sent then as an argument. This message send returns an integer object 154.

Both the message sends in this expression are binary. According to the order of evaluation, the $+$ message is sent first, then the $*$ message. In Smalltalk all arithmetic expressions are evaluated according to the order of evaluation. In some cases the result differs from the conventional arithmetic order of evaluation.

Oh, I see. I will remember that and improve my Smalltalk code reading habits. Thank you.

How about doing some more arithmetic for me?

What would you like me to do?

$F = C (1.8) + 32$
Where $C = 20$.

Code	Returned Value
`C := 20.` `F := C * (1.8) + 32.`	68

$A^2 + B^2$
Where $A = 7$ and $B = 9$.

Code	Returned Value
`7 squared + 9 squared.`	130

$\tan^{-1}(\cos(X) + \sin(1-X))$

Where X = 0.6 radians.

Code	Returned Value
```| x |```	
```x := 0.6.```	
```(x cos + (1-x) sin)```	
``` arcTan.```	0.882061

How about doing that for X = 45 degrees?

Code	Returned Value
```| x |```	
```x := 45 degreesToRadians.```	
```(x cos + (1-x) sin)```	
``` arcTan.```	0.882061

If you want the answer in degrees, use the radiansToDegrees message.

n! / r!
For five things (n) taken three (r) at a time.

Code	Returned Value
```| n r |```	
```n := 5.```	
```r := 3.```	
```n factorial /```	
``` r factorial.```	20

Hmmm, not bad. Tell me more about the individual subclasses of class Number.

Class `Float` implements the arithmetic operations on floating-point numbers. The precision of floating-point numbers in Smalltalk depends upon your hardware and operating system. Check your Smalltalk/V reference manual and your hardware for the real answer.

Class `Integer` implements the arithmetic operations on integer numbers. Actually `Integer` is an abstract class with three subclasses: `LargePositiveInteger`, `LargeNegativeInteger`, and `SmallInteger`. It is OK to forget this: the conversion between the different kinds of integers is automatic.

Integers in Smalltalk can get quite large. Try this piece of code, which computes the factorial of 100:

```
| answer |
answer := 1.
1 to: 100 do: [:num |
    answer := answer * num].
^answer.
```

This returns a large integer. To see how large, replace the last line with:

```
^answer printString size.
```

This returns the number of digits in the answer.

Class `Fraction` implements the arithmetic operations on rational numbers (fractions). Since the numerator and denominator are both represented as integers, fractions can be very precise—much more precise than the hardware-based floating-point numbers.

Are there any heuristics for learning to use arithmetic in Smalltalk?

Yes:

1. Remember that there are unary, binary, and keyword messages in the Number classes, and the type of message sent affects the order of evaluation. When in doubt, use parentheses.
2. Mixed-mode arithmetic is allowed. The result is determined by the arithmetic functions used. Usually the answer moves to the most general kind of number in the expression, with fractions more general than integers and floats more general than integers or fractions.
3. The arithmetic capabilities of the system are extensible. In other words, if a capability does not exist, you can create it.
4. Floating-point math is coprocessor based; a software floating-point capability is available, however, for all versions of Smalltalk/V.

I think I've got it. I'm ready to write some code.

Then I will see you later. Do not forget the To Do tasks for this chapter.

Summary

New Terms

Rational Number (Fraction)

What Did You Learn?

Arithmetic in Smalltalk is similar to but different from arithmetic in other
languages.
The normal Smalltalk order of execution is used for arithmetic.
Parentheses help make arithmetic expressions more readable.
The mathematical operations are implemented in Smalltalk methods.
The mathematical operations are changeable and extensible.
New number systems can be implemented with new subclasses of Number.
Implementing numeric expressions in Smalltalk is a piece of cake.
The message interface to the Number classes is extensive.

Words of Wisdom

Remember the order of execution, or subtle bugs can creep into your code. If you're
not sure, use parentheses.

There is nothing sacred about the methods in the Number classes. If you have a
good reason to add one, then add it.

To Do List

Write a method in Number that will answer the receiver incremented by 1. Write a
similar method that will decrement the receiver by 1.

You work for NASA (National Aeronautics and Space Administration). Your job is
multidimensional software support:

1. You must extend the math capabilities of Smalltalk to meet NASA needs.

2. You must implement selected formulas in Smalltalk.

3. You must create tools for the local applied mathematicians and physicists.

Your first requests for extending the mathematical capabilities of Smalltalk involve adding some unit conversion methods:

`fahrenheitToKelvin`	Answer degrees Kelvin from Fahrenheit
`lightYearsToMillimeters`	Answer millimeters from light-years
`yearsToSeconds`	Answer seconds from years

The speed of light is about 3.0×10^{10} centimeters per second. The Kelvin temperature scale uses the same degree size as Centigrade, but the 0 point for Kelvin is absolute zero ($-273°$ C).

A new laser-based system has been installed at NASA to provide communications with space probes and exploration platforms. Write some Smalltalk code that will answer the round-trip speed-of-light communications delay. Specify some space objects that are interesting distances from Earth. As a test, you should get a delay of about 2.567 seconds for communicating with Tyco Moonbase (384,068 kilometers away). Question: Should the returned object be an instance of `Time`?

Engineers are asking for an extension to the `Number` classes to handle complex numbers. Design such a system by creating a class definition and a message interface list. If you have time, start on the implementation. Remember that complex numbers have an imaginary and a real part, just as fractions have a numerator and denominator.

5

DEBUGGING AND TESTING

Contents at: 'Chapter 5'

Questions Of Interest

What are Smalltalk code errors like?

Do conventional debugging strategies work?

Where does the walkback come from?

How is the debugger used?

Introduction

Debugging and testing Smalltalk code in some ways is similar to debugging and testing procedural code; in other ways it is new and different. In any case, this chapter does not represent the last word on object-oriented debugging and testing.

All debugging processes begin with an event called an "error." In this chapter you will learn the nature of an object-oriented error, where it is detected, and how it is reported to the programmer. As you will see, errors can be reported from the compiler during compilation, from the virtual machine, and from Smalltalk code during run-time.

Goals for this Chapter

To learn about Smalltalk errors, how to find them, and what to do after you find them.

To evaluate the performance of Smalltalk code.

Jim   **Objective Wizard**

Hey, I need help!

> Why? What is going on?

Well, I've started to write
code, and I have errors.

> What do you want me to do?

Fix them. Or at least teach
me how to deal with them.

> Debugging is an important part of Smalltalk pro-
> gramming, so let us talk about it in some detail.
>
> How would you like to start?

Error reports are popping up
on my screen, and I don't know
what they mean. I'm having
problems understanding what
constitutes a Smalltalk error
and how the error is reported
to me.

I'm getting frustrated.

Where's my Fortran compiler?

> Jim, buddy, relax!
>
> Insert this method in your message interface and
> send it to yourself:

```
relax
    "Set physiological parameters
    to relax level"
self bloodPressure: 120/80.
self heartRate: 70.
```

You will feel better soon. I never know when to tell humans about Smalltalk debugging. If I tell them too early, they cannot understand its usefulness. If I tell them too late, they have an error attack, like you just had.

Sit back, relax, and listen.

Smalltalk errors can be conveniently categorized by understanding when the error is detected and whence the error report is generated.

There are three sources for error reporting in Smalltalk:

1. virtual machine
2. `Compiler`
3. Smalltalk code

The virtual machine reports a `doesNotUnderstand:` whenever a receiver object is sent a message that is not in its local or inherited message interface. The virtual machine also reports a `controlBreak`. Both messages are generated during run-time and are reported to the programmer via the walkback window, Smalltalk's run-time error reporting mechanism.

The compiler reports errors during compilation—in other words, whenever you execute code with a "show it" or "do it" or you save a method in the class hierarchy browser or with another tool. The compiler inserts a small error message in reverse video into your code at the point the error was detected.

Smalltalk code also can report an error condition. Although the programmer has little control over the messages reported by the compiler or virtual machine, messages reported from Smalltalk code can be modified, added, or removed.

Let's begin with the compiler errors. I get those all the time.

All right, Jim. Examples of typical compiler
errors are:

```
invalid receiver
should be selector
missing "]"
missing ")"
unfinished comment
undefined
```

Compiler errors are generally related to syntax
problems. To debug a compiler error:

1. Read the error message.
2. Look at where it was inserted. The error
   lies either immediately before or after the
   error message.
3. Identify the error. Press the delete or
   backspace key to eliminate the error message, and then fix the code.

If you cannot find the problem, try these techniques:

1. Comment out a small chunk of code, then
   compile it again to isolate the error.
2. Check your code for missing end-of-state-
   ment periods, missing receiver objects, and
   typos in variable names.

When all else fails, ask someone else to look at
your code. The simplest errors are often the most
difficult to find!

What about the errors that
happen at run-time and pop
up a walkback window?

The `error:` method inherited from `Object` reports error conditions from Smalltalk code. A list of
the methods that send the `error:` message can be
seen by selecting `error:` in a class hierarchy

browser and using the "senders" option on the methods menu.

All error messages reported from Smalltalk code using the `error:` method will display a walkback window.

Very interesting, but what do I do with a walkback when I get one?

A *walkback* is a Smalltalk window handled by an instance of `Debugger`. It represents two very important pieces of information:

1. Your code has encountered an error condition.
2. The walkback window's title area has an error message, which may provide you with the solution to the problem. In many cases, particularly with the `doesNotUnderstand:` error, the walkback provides all the information you need.

The walkback window also contains a view into the Smalltalk execution stack. If you depress the control and break keys on your keyboard, a walkback window is displayed. The main part of the window would look like:

Process class >> controlBreakInterrupt
Process class (Object) >> perform:
True (Object) >> vmInterrupt:
ProcessScheduler >> schedule

Each line of the stack information can be read as some message send to some object. For example, the first line reads: the `controlBreakInterrupt` message was sent to the class `Process`. The second line reads: the `perform:` message was sent to the class `Process`, and the `perform:` message is inherited from the class

`Object`. Displaying the name of the class from which the message is inherited makes it easy to find the method when you need more information.

So how does the information in the walkback window help me fix the error?

Start at the top line of the execution stack information and work your way down. The first method listed that you wrote is usually where the error occurred. This tends to be the second or third line, but it may be much farther down.

I see. Anything else?

When a walkback window is displayed, you have three options:

1. Solve the problem with information provided by the walkback, close the walkback, and fix the problem.
2. Resume execution from the walkback by selecting the "resume" option from the walkback menu. You can resume only from control break and halt encountered errors.
3. Select the "debug" option in the walkback window and use the debugger to help you solve the problem.

Thanks, I feel as if I can do something now when I get an error condition.

What can you tell me about using the debugger?

The `Debugger` is a multipane, window-based application that provides you with a group of tools for exploring the code around the reported error.

The Smalltalk/V tutorial describes the `Debugger` better than I can in this low-bandwidth style of communication. When you are familiar with the `Debugger`, try surprising some object with a control break, and then use the debugger to see what that object was doing.

All right, I'll look at the debugger tutorial when I get back to the office. What else can you tell me about debugging in Smalltalk?

How about a few common debugging techniques, such as:

1. embedding code
2. separate testing
3. stub objects
4. message recorders

Sounds interesting. Would you include some code examples?

Sure. *Embedding code* in a method to make code participate in its own debugging is like embedding debugging code in a procedure or function in any other language.

With embedded code in Smalltalk you can:

1. Halt the execution at a point in the code.

   ```
   self halt.
   ```

2. Make a noise every time a particular method or statement is executed.

   ```
   Terminal bell.
   ```

3. Write a string to the `Transcript` window.

```
Transcript
    nextPutAll: 'some string'; cr.
```

4. Keep track of a particular variable or piece of data. Use a global variable to store the value, and then look at it after the fact.

What do you mean by "separate testing?"

Separate testing means testing each class as you build it. By doing this you ensure each individual class (and its instances) work correctly before you combine them into an application.

When I start a new class, I open a workspace, in which I put the debugging code and notes until I am finished with the class. This provides a sort of running commentary on my development-testing process.

That seems pretty intuitive. What is a "stub object?"

A *stub object* is an object whose message interface is identical (or at least similar) to some complex object you have not finished. You can test the code that uses that object before you are ready to finish it.

I don't get it. Isn't it as difficult to create the stub object as it is to create the object you haven't finished?

Not necessarily. The stub object's methods might return default values or even prompt you for the correct answer.

Hmmm. Is it possible to implement a generic stub class?

Yes, it is possible, Jim, but not easy. I suggest that you wait until you have mastered more of Smalltalk before you try.

Oh, well, in that case why don't you tell me about message recorders?

Message recorders simply record what messages they receive. By studying the list of messages, you can learn how an object is used. This is particularly useful in a multiperson development environment.

Unfortunately, creating a generic message recorder requires knowledge and techniques you do not have yet. You can create a partial message recorder by having the messages in which you are interested write a message to the transcript window.

So I really can't do either generic stub objects or message recorders now?

Correct. They both require the ability to build a generic encapsulator, or something like it, which requires that you add the message `addSubclass:` to `UndefinedObject` or modify a method in `MetaClass` so . . . .

Yow! Hold on! I believe you.

Before I leave, could you give me some ideas about performance testing and code optimization?

First, implement a performance tester to collect

data on the execution of particular code segments. Try this chunk of code:

```
Time millisecondsToRun: [
    1000 timesRepeat: [
        code to test ]]
```

This will answer the number of milliseconds required to execute the code to test 1000 times. The timing precision is limited to the resolution of the system clock.

And how do I change my code to improve performance?

Smalltalk executes faster than you might suppose. In my strategy, I wait until toward the end of development. Only after I have data that indicates there is a problem do I concern myself about performance details.

Specific changes are tied to specific code, but in general:

1. Always gather statistics to help locate a performance problem.
2. Focus on optimizing code that gets executed a lot.
3. Caching (keeping available rather than throwing out) graphics images and disk file information can reduce the processing overhead.
4. Sometimes it helps to change which collection you use to track groups of objects. Certain collections are fast at certain tasks. For example, an instance of Set executes includes: messages very quickly, even over large numbers of objects.
5. The kind of number you use can make a big difference. Floating-point numbers are fast if your system has a coprocessor, but slow if it does not.

Thanks, Wiz. Adiós.

Vamos a la playa.

No, gracias.

Adiós.

Summary

New Terms

Walkback

Debugger

What Did You Learn?

Errors are reported by the `Compiler`, virtual machine, and from Smalltalk code.

The `error:` message reports errors from Smalltalk code.

The heuristics for resolving compiler errors.

Debugging techniques for Smalltalk are similar to those for conventional languages.

Words of Wisdom

Test as you go. Testing a class as you build it saves time and trouble later.

First make it work, then make it fast. Optimizing code as you write it wastes time by optimizing code that doesn't need it.

Code is never correct the first time. We not only should accept and get accustomed to this, but use it. Iterative refinement gives you a way to turn this to your advantage.

Read the information in a walkback window. It is important!

Use a timer to evaluate code performance.

There are several basic heuristics for increasing code performance.

To Do List

Find the debugging chapter in the Smalltalk/V manual. Read it carefully.

Insert the following code in the beginning of a method you want to observe:

```
self halt.
```

One interesting method is `asLowerCase` in `String`.

Send the message that activates the method you have changed. This should open up a walkback window. Use the walkback menu to open the debugger.

Spend some time poking around the code and playing with the debugger. Get familiar with this tool, as you will be spending a lot of time with it. List all the debugger's menu options, and then find out what they do. Write a line or two about each and put it up on your wall.

As you read the next couple of chapters, you should find ample opportunity to use the walkback window and debugger. Be careful; it's easy to get addicted to a good interactive debugging system.

6

COLLECTIONS

Contents at: 'Chapter 6'

```
#(
the primary collection hierarchy
    Collection
        Bag
        IndexedCollection
            FixedSizeCollection
                Array
                ByteArray
                Interval
                String
                OrderedCollection
                    SortedCollection
            Set
                Dictionary
criteria for comparing collections
    size
    indexing
    access
    adding and removing
    multiple occurrences
    syntax, restrictions, and capabilities
conversion messages
Stream)
```

Questions Of Interest

How can I store and manipulate objects?
How do I create a container?
How do I put things into my container?
Can I change containers?
Can I make a new kind of container?
Why would I want to?

Introduction

Smalltalk supports a rich set of collections. The polymorphic nature of Smalltalk and lack of data typing makes the collections truly generic. The collections don't need to be reimplemented for every kind of object they contain.

Because collections have a common message interface, you don't need to choose which collection to use until you know more about the needs of the user and application code. This capability allows simple initial implementations to become more complex when appropriate.

Conversion messages, another capability of the `Collection` hierarchy, allow you to easily convert one type of collection to another and then back again.

Goals for this Chapter

To know what collections are implemented in Smalltalk and where to find them.

To understand the capabilities and limitations of the more common collections well enough to choose which is needed.

To understand how collections differ.

To use collections in your own applications.

Jim	**Objective Wizard**

Hey, Wiz, I have an emergency. Can you help me?

Certainly. I have been waiting for you. I was concerned that you had quit before I could tell you about collections in Smalltalk.

Well, data structures are the reason I'm here. Much of my work revolves around the containment and manipulation of data.

In Smalltalk the interesting data structures are implemented as subclasses of `Collection`, so instead of talking about data structures, we talk about collections.

Sounds like what I want.

Then hold on to your keyboard, buddy. Smalltalk has a really interesting array (pun intended) of collections. Here is the `Collection` hierarchy:

```
Collection
    Bag
    IndexedCollection
        FixedSizeCollection
            Array
            ByteArray
            Interval
            String
        OrderedCollection
            SortedCollection
    Set
    Dictionary
```

All these classes are collections in the sense that they contain and manipulate objects. Each subclass is either a data structure for your use or a holder of functionality to be inherited. `Collection`, `IndexedCollection`, and `FixedSizeCollection` are abstract classes, which you will not use directly. All the other classes listed above will be useful. Some, however, will be used soon and often, so we will cover those first.

After I point out what they have in common, I will talk about each separately with examples.

Sounds great! I'm all ears.

The collection classes have a common message interface, meaning there is a set of messages every collection can handle. As a result, you do not have to know which collection you are dealing with to use them.

First I want to mention the iteration messages, which give you a way to execute a piece of code for each element in the collection. The messages are:

```
do:
select:
reject:
collect:
detect:
inject:into:
```

We will discuss these in Chapter 7.

There also are some messages that test whether a particular object is in a collection:

```
includes:
occurrencesOf:
```

The `includes:` answers true if the collection contains at least one occurrence of the object passed as an argument. The `occurrencesOf:` message answers how many occurrences of the object passed as an argument are in the collection.

Some messages will tell you about the collection as a whole:

```
isEmpty
notEmpty
size
```

The `isEmpty` and `notEmpty` messages will answer true and false, respectively, if the collection has no elements. The `size` message will answer the number of elements in the collection.

These messages work for any collection?

Yes, even those we do not discuss.

The subclasses of `Collection` we will discuss are:

```
Bag
Array
String
OrderedCollection
SortedCollection
Set
Dictionary
```

That's a lot of collections. How will I decide which one to use?

There are some good comparison criteria that will help you.

Great. What are they?

Ask yourself the following questions:

1. Do I need a fixed or variable size collection? In other words, do I want my collec-

tion to grow as more data is added, or do I want it to stay the same size?

2. Do I need an indexed data structure? In other words, do I want to index into my data structure to reach the object at some location?

3. How do I want to access my data objects? This is tied to indexing, for a collection that cannot be indexed allows few ways to find out what is in it.

4. How do I want to add and remove objects from my data structure? I have many choices here. Most important, do I want to toss objects into the collection or do I want to put them in specific places?

5. Do I want to store multiple occurrences of an object in my data structure? In other words, do I want to add the same object more than once?

6. Are there any special capabilities or restrictions I should take into account?

Let's start with `Bag`!

Class `Bag` is modeled after a physical bag, like the kind you get in a grocery store. You can put things into and take things out of a bag, but there is no real structure. A Bag is just a clump of objects with no particular organization.

Here is how a `Bag` stacks up with our criteria:

Questions	Answers
Fixed Size?	No
Indexed?	No
Access?	None
Add & Remove?	`add:`, `remove:`
Multiple Occurrences?	Yes

Here is an example. A bag used as a sales monitor in a music store holds all the day's sales:

```
SaleMonitor := Bag new.
```

Sales personnel add sales to the bag:

```
SaleMonitor
    add: 'Jimmy Buffett';
    add: 'Bach';
    add: 'Jimmy Buffett';
    add: 'Hank Snow';
    add: 'Cindy Lauper'.
```

To ask how many sales were made today, type:

```
SaleMonitor size.
```

To ask how many Jimmy Buffett CDs sold today, type:

```
SaleMonitor
    occurrencesOf: 'Jimmy Buffett'.
```

To ask if there were any sales today, type:

```
SaleMonitor notEmpty.
```

What's next?

Class `Array`. It is very similar to the conventional implementation of an array. In Smalltalk an `Array` is a collection with a fixed number of places where you can insert objects, like an egg carton.

Here are vital statistics of `Array`:

Questions	Answers
Fixed Size?	Yes
Indexed?	Yes
Access?	at:, first, last
Add & Remove?	at:put:
Multiple Occurrences?	Yes

I've worked with arrays in other languages. But it seems that arrays in Smalltalk can hold any kind of object.

Say, does that mean I can put collections inside other collections?

> Yes. Any object really means any object. You can even put a collection inside itself.

Weird.

> It is perfectly natural to residents of ObjectLand. Soon it will be second nature to you, too.
>
> Let us make an instance of `Array` and experiment.
>
> ```
> A := Array new: 4.
> ```
>
> We have created an array that can contain four objects. To put some objects in the array, we will use the `at:put:` message.
>
> ```
> A    at: 1 put: 100;
>      at: 2 put: 200;
>      at: 3 put: 'Hi';
>      at: 4 put: 'There'.
> ```
>
> I have a question for you, Jim. What was in the array before we executed this last piece of code?

Hmm . . . I'm not sure. I would guess there was nothing in it.

> Sorry, Jim. Any variable, or any element in an array, that has not yet been assigned, or set a value with an `at:put:` message, contains the `nil` object. This holds true for most fixed size collections.

Most?

Yes, some collections can contain only particular kinds of objects. For example, a `ByteArray` can contain only the integers from 0 to 255, while instances of `String` can contain only characters. To see what these classes use as default values, type:

```
(ByteArray new: 4) at: 1.
(String new: 4) at: 1.
```

I'll try that when I get back to the office.

Now that we have an array, let us send it some messages:

Code	Returned Value
A at: 3.	'Hi'
A isEmpty.	false
A size.	4
A includes: 99.	false
A occurrencesOf: 'Hi'.	1
A at: 2 put: 99.	99
A last.	'There'
A at: 2.	99

I should remind you of something we talked about in Chapter 2. An instance of `Array` can be created by using a shortcut syntax. We could have created and initialized our original array by doing this:

```
A := #(100 200 'Hi' 'There').
```

I don't normally think of strings as data structures.

Didn't you say they could
contain only characters?

Yes, I did. Instances of `String` are like arrays that contain only characters. Strings have
a sort of split personality. From one point of
view a string is a collection with all the normal
collection behaviors. From another point of
view a string is an object with a message interface designed for dealing with strings.
Smalltalk handles this dichotomy by making
`String` a subclass of `Collection`, and then
enhancing it with a special syntax and a lot of
extra messages.

Here is how `String` fits into our criteria:

Questions	Answers
Fixed Size?	Yes
Indexed?	Yes
Access?	at:, first, last
Add & Remove?	at:put:
Multiple Occurrences?	Yes
Restriction?	Characters only

So strings are like arrays with
extra string-handling messages. Could you show me
some of those extra mes-
sages?

Certainly.

Code	Returned Value
`'abcd' asUpperCase`	`'ABCD'`
`'AMBER' reversed`	`'REBMA'`
`'-47' asInteger`	`-47`
`'Hi' >= 'Ho'`	`false`
`'12 Oct 1492' asDate`	`Oct 12, 1492`

Now let us do some code that treats a string as
a collection.

```
A := String new: 4.
A    at: 1 put: $h;
     at: 2 put: $o;
     at: 3 put: $m;
     at: 4 put: $e.
```

Code	Returned Value
A at: 3	$m
A at: 1 put: $d	$d
A first	$d
A includes: $K	false
A occurrencesOf: $o	1
A size	4

Interesting! I can switch between treating strings as strings
and treating them as collections. That could be handy.

All right, I'm ready for the
next one.

Instead of one, I will give you two examples and
cover both OrderedCollection, the most generally useful collection in ObjectLand, and SortedCollection.

OrderedCollection is like an array that
grows as large as you need. You can increase its
size by adding new objects to the front or back of
the collection.

SortedCollection is the same, except the
order is determined by a sorting strategy.

Here is the basic information for Ordered-
Collection:

Questions	Answers
Fixed Size?	No
Indexed?	Yes
Access?	at:, first, last
Add & Remove?	at:put:, add:, remove:
Multiple Occurrences?	Yes

The basics for `SortedCollection` are similar:

Questions	Answers
Fixed Size?	No
Indexed?	Yes
Access?	at:, first, last
Add & Remove?	add:, remove:
Multiple Occurrences?	Yes
Capability?	Sorting
Restriction?	Sorting strategy

Why is "sorting strategy" a restriction?

Sorted collections use something called a "sort block" to decide whether two objects are in the correct order. The default sort block uses the `<=` message. If you try to add an object that the sort block cannot handle, you will get a walkback window signaling an error.

So I have to be certain that the objects in the sorted collection can handle the `<=` message; otherwise I need to create a new sort block.

How do I create a sort block?

Sort blocks are two argument blocks that answer true if the first and second arguments are in the correct order, and false if they are not. We will discuss blocks in Chapter 7.

How about some examples?

Fine.

Let us begin by creating one of each collection:

```
A := OrderedCollection new.
S := SortedCollection new.
```

Code	Returned Value
A add: 10.	10
A add: 11.	11
A addFirst: 44.	44
A asArray.	(44 10 11)
A first.	44
S addAll: A.	
S asArray.	(10 11 44)
A at: 2 put: 1.	1
A removeFirst	44
S addAll: A.	
S asArray.	(1 10 11 11 44)
S removeFirst.	1

That asArray message looks interesting. Are there any others like it?

Yes. I will talk about them after we cover the other collections.

Sets are next, aren't they? Are they anything like the sets I learned about in my math classes?

Yes and yes. Instances of Set act much the same as the sets you learned about in school. Unfortunately they do not include the set operations, such as union and intersection. You, however, can create those yourself.

It seems as if I can change anything I don't like about Smalltalk. That alone is worth the trip to ObjectLand.

I am glad you feel that way. Most of Smalltalk is written in itself, with the source code available. Just be careful to make backup copies before initiating any major changes.

Here is the basic information for `Set`:

Questions	Answers
Fixed Size?	No
Indexed?	No
Access?	None
Add & Remove?	`add:`, `remove:`
Multiple Occurrences?	No

Note that sets will not contain multiple occurrences of an object. For example:

Code	Returned Value
`A := Set new`	`Set ()`
`A add: 10.`	`10`
`A add: 9.`	`9`
`A add: 10.`	`10`
`A size.`	`2`
`A.`	`Set (10 9)`

Oh. Sets are like bags, except they don't keep multiple occurrences. Does that mean the `occurrencesOf:` mes-

sage always answers 1 when
sent to a set?

> An excellent question! The `occurrencesOf:`
> message will always answer 1 if the argument is in
> the set, 0 if it is not.

What's next?

> `Dictionary` is very interesting. Unlike the other
> collections, `Dictionary` stores sets of relation-
> ships between two objects. Once the relationship
> has been entered, you can access a value object if
> you know the associated key object.
>
> Here is our criteria information:

Questions	Answers
Fixed Size?	No
Indexed?	Yes (any object)
Access?	`at:`
Add & Remove?	`at:put:`, `removeKey:`
Multiple Occurrences?	No for keys Yes for values

I'm not sure I understand.

> It is easier to show you.

```
D := Dictionary new.
```

Code	Returned Value
`D at: 'one' put: 1.`	`1`
`D at: 'two' put: 2.`	`2`
`D at: 'zero' put: 0.`	`0`
`D at: 1 put: 'one'.`	`'one'`
`D at: 2 put: 'two'.`	`'two'`

```
D size.                     5
D at: 2.                    'two'
D at: 'two'.                2
D occurrencesOf: 2.         1
D removeKey: 'one'.
D size.                     4
```

With an instance of class Dictionary, when you talk about one of the objects it contains, you talk about a value not a key. So messages such as includes: and do: apply only to the values in the dictionary.

You were going to say more about asArray and similar messages.

You can switch easily between collections with a *conversion message,* which copies the collection to which it is sent, and translates it into a different kind of collection. The copied collection takes on the attributes of the new collection. For example:

Code	Returned Value
'Hello' size.	5
'Hello' asSet size.	4
'Hi' asArray.	($H $i)
#(1 2 3 2 1) asSet.	Set(3 2 1)

Converting a collection to a set squishes out all the duplicates. Similar things happen when converting to other kinds of collections. Here are the collection conversion messages included in Smalltalk (of course, you can add more if you wish):

```
asArray
asBag
asOrderedCollection
asSet
asSortedCollection
```

Neat! Now I know how to contain and organize my information, but why isn't there a way
to store data in a disk file?

But there is, Jim.

What is it, Wizard?

There are several classes involved when storing
data in files. But we must discuss Stream and its
subclasses first.

You can think of a stream as a collection with another point of view. It does several collectionlike
things, including containing groups of objects and
preserving an order within that group. But a
stream's intent is different than that of a collection.
A stream has a more dynamic view of data than
does a collection.

Each stream works with a collection; we call this
"streaming over a collection." The stream keeps
track of a position within the collection, and that
position controls what part of the collection it affects when you send the stream messages.

An example:

```
S := ReadWriteStream on: #(1 2).
```

Code	Returned Value
S next.	1
S next.	2
S atEnd.	true
S reset.	
S next.	1
S position.	1
S nextPut: 7.	7
S nextPut: 8.	8
S contents.	(1 7 8)
S nextPutAll: 'AB'.	'AB'
S contents.	(1 7 8 $A $B)

As you can see, streams work with one position of their underlying collection at a time. They also have messages that examine their current position, and they can change their current position. There are many more messages; use a class hierarchy browser to look at more of the `Stream` message interface.

But what does this have to do with disk files?

Let me show you the `Stream` class hierarchy:

```
Stream
    ReadStream
    WriteStream
        ReadWriteStream
        FileStream
```

The last class, `FileStream`, should interest you. Instead of working with an underlying collection, file streams use an underlying disk file.

`FileStreams` are a little different from other streams: they can handle only characters, and they also have several messages that do not apply to other `Stream` subclasses (for example, the message `close`).

To create a file stream and at the same time open (or create) a file, send the `pathName:` class message to `File`.

```
S := File pathName: 'MyFile.txt'.
```

The argument to the `pathName:` message can be a fully qualified path name.

You now have a file stream over an open file with the position set at the beginning of the file (which is zero). You can send any of the stream messages to read, write, or modify the file contents. When you are done working with the file, do this:

```
S close.
```

This closes the file, cleaning up any necessary odds and ends.

To find out more about files, look at the class methods in the classes `File` and `Directory` and the instance methods in the class `FileStream`.

Good. I think I can figure out the disk file stuff now. I'd better go now. My brain is full.

All right. Goodbye for now.

Do not forget the To Do List.

Summary

New Terms

Collection	Stream
Set	File Stream
Conversion Messages	Disk File

What Did You Learn?

Many of the data structure capabilities of Smalltalk are in the `Collection` classes.

There is a set of criteria to help select a collection.

Conversion messages create new kinds of collections from existing ones.

More can be learned about collections, streams, and disk files in Smalltalk by exploring the message interface to each.

Words of Wisdom

It's usually better to have a collection than to be one. Most of the time it's better to have an instance variable that contains a collection than to be a subclass of a collection—even if it's your only instance variable.

You will spend much of your implementation time picking and using collections. It pays to learn about them and understand how they work. To learn, explore the message interfaces, and then experiment by sending messages to an instance of a collection.

Collection Summary

Collection Comparison Table

Class Name	Indexed	Fixed Size	Duplicates
Array	Yes	Yes	Yes
Bag	No	No	Yes
Dictionary	Yes (1)	No	Yes (1)
OrderedCollection	Yes	No	Yes
Set	No	No	No
SortedCollection (2)	Yes	No	Yes
String (3)	Yes	Yes	Yes

(1) Instances of Dictionary are indexed by any object. The index objects (keys) cannot have duplicates, but the values associated with them may.

(2) Instances of SortedCollection keep their contents in a sorted order, defined by the sort block. The default sort block uses the <= message. The sort block may restrict which objects may be added to a given instance of SortedCollection.

(3) Instances of String may contain only character objects.

Common Message Interface

do:	Repeat a piece of code for each element.
collect:	Map each element into a new collection.
select:	Filter some elements into a new collection.
reject:	Filter an element out; put the rest into a new collection.
occurrencesOf:	Answer the number of occurrences of the argument.
includes:	Answer true if the argument is in the collection.
isEmpty	Answer true if the collection has no elements.
notEmpty	Answer true if the collection has elements.
size	Answer the number of elements in the collection.

To Do List

Create a class called Stack that implements a normal set of stack operations. For now, make it a subclass of Object. The message interface should include:

`push:` anObject	Put anObject on the top of the stack.
`pop`	Answer the object on top of the stack after removing it.
`size`	Answer the number of elements in the stack.
`isEmpty`	Answer true if the stack is empty; else, answer false.
`clear`	Clear the stack.

There is a programming trick that initializes an object's instance variables as soon as it is created. You may find it useful for the `Stack` class. You can find an example in the class method `new` and in the instance method `initialize`; both are in class `Bag`.

Implement a class called `SalesRecorder` that supports the entry of sales information. Initially sales information is limited to the product sold, but you may wish to make enhancements later. Here is a possible message interface:

`addSale:` aProduct	Add the sale of the product aProduct.
`salesOf:` aProduct	Answer the number of sales of aProduct.
`totalSales`	Answer the total number of sales.
`clear`	Clear all sales data.

To start, use strings to name your products.

Extra Credit

Use the `Prompter` and `Menu` (or `MessageBox`) `message:` message to build a user interface to your sales recorder.

Create a class called `Product` and integrate it with your sales recorder application.

Keep track of sales by day, week, and month.

7

BOOLEANS AND BLOCKS

Contents at: 'Chapter 7'

```
#(
boolean
    true
    false
boolean combinations
boolean comparisons
conditional execution
    ifTrue: ifFalse:
blocks
more conditional execution
    [ ] whileTrue: [ ]
    [ ] whileFalse: [ ]
basic iteration
    timesRepeat: [ ]
    to: do: [:var| ]
    to: by: do: [:var| ]
collection iteration
    do:
    collect:
    select:
    reject:)
```

Questions of Interest

What are Smalltalk's boolean capabilities?
What conditional statements can I use?
What is a block and how can I use it?
What iterators are available?

Introduction

In Chapter 2 you saw that there are no conditional or iteration constructs in the core language. These capabilities are implemented as classes, instances, and methods in the class hierarchy, allowing you to change and enhance the basic conditional and iteration constructs.

A block, this chapter's hardest concept, is a chunk of code that is stuffed into an object rather than executed, allowing the code to be executed, more than once if necessary, by sending a message to the block object.

Goals for this Chapter

To understand what it means for booleans (true and false) to be objects.
To write code using boolean combinations.
To write code using comparison messages.
To know and to use the available conditional messages.
To understand the different ways to do iteration in Smalltalk.
To understand how to use blocks.

Jim   **Objective Wizard**

Hi, I'm back.

> Greetings, Human. This time we will talk about some very important constructs.

You mean there's more to learn?

> That, Jim, is an understatement. At the moment I want to discuss how to use booleans, blocks, conditional statements, and iterators in your code.

Yeah, I've been wondering about those.

> Good, I want to start with booleans. Is your brain booted?

I am a human. My brain does not boot.

> Yes, I have heard that said about humans.

How are boolean capabilities implemented in Smalltalk?

> Boolean capabilities in Smalltalk are implemented in the abstract class `Boolean` and its subclasses `True` and `False`. The boolean values we use in our code are instances of `True` and `False`. The instance of `True` can be referenced using the pseudo variable `true`; the instance of `False` can be referenced through the pseudo variable `false`.

Very interesting implementation. How do I combine booleans?

The boolean operators *and, or, not, exclusive or,* and *equivalence* are implemented in the classes True and False. Here are the messages used to do these operations:

Operation	Message	Argument
and	&	aBoolean
and	and:	aBlock
or			aBoolean
or	or:	aBlock
not	not	none
exclusive or	xor:	aBoolean
equivalence	eqv:	aBoolean

Note that the and operation has both a binary message (&) and a keyword message (and:). The binary message always evaluates the code that answers its argument boolean. The keyword message takes an unevaluated piece of code as its argument, evaluating it only if it must.

The same holds true for the or operation.

I'm not sure I understand the difference between & and and:, how about an example?

Certainly. Execute the following piece of code:

```
| x |
x := nil.
x notNil & (x > 0)
    ifFalse: [Terminal bell].
```

You get a "does not understand" error because nil does not handle the > message. The code (x > 0) executed because the & message simply takes two boolean values as arguments.

The and: message takes an unevaluated piece of code as an argument, executing it only if it must. The following piece of code works correctly:

```
| x |
x := nil.
(x notNil and: [x > 0])
    ifFalse: [Terminal bell].
```

Here the code `[x > 0]` is not executed, so there is no error.

I think I understand. Square brackets insure that the code doesn't execute right away.

Correct. It is a block. We will discuss it in more detail later in the chapter.

How do you compare and test objects?

You compare and test objects with a comparison message. In Smalltalk a *comparison message* is any message that answers either true or false. Here are some common comparison messages:

Operation	Message
equal	=
not equal	~=
greater than	>
less than	<
is odd number	odd
is even number	even
is the nil object	isNil
is not the nil object	notNil
exactly equal	==
not exactly equal	~~

Every object either implements or inherits the messages isNil, notNil, =, ~=, ==, and ~~. These messages work with any object.

Well, except for that weird

stuff with the pseudo variables `true` and `false`,
booleans in Smalltalk are
similar to what I'm used to.

What about some conditional
statements?

Smalltalk's *conditional statements* simply are messages to a boolean object:

```
ifTrue:ifFalse:
ifFalse:ifTrue:
ifTrue:
ifFalse:
```

These are all the possible combinations of
`ifTrue:` and `ifFalse:`. The arguments for
these messages are zero argument blocks, which
are pieces of code that have not been executed.

Does this make sense, Jim?

I understand everything except that block thing. Some
examples would help.

Implemented in the class `Context` and its subclasses, a block is one or more Smalltalk expressions surrounded by brackets [   ]. Blocks are
used throughout the system, particularly in conditional and iteration statements. For example:

```
(5 odd) ifTrue: [Terminal bell].
```

In this expression the `ifTrue:` message was sent
to the object returned from the `(5 odd)` expression. In this case a true is returned from `(5
odd)`, and as a result, the `ifTrue:` method exe-
cutes the block of code `[Terminal bell]` by
sending the block the `value` message.

Here are more examples:

```
count isNil
   ifTrue: [count := 1]
   ifFalse: [count := count + 1].
```

ifTrue:ifFalse, like every other message,
returns a value. In this case the value comes from
the piece of code that gets evaluated. The last
example could be rewritten:

```
count :=
   count isNil
      ifTrue: [1]
      ifFalse: [count + 1].
```

The only meaningful difference is that of style.

One more example:

```
count > 10000 ifTrue: [
   count := 0.
   list := OrderedCollection new.
   ^self error:
      'Overflow problem'].
```

OK, I'm sure I understand the
testing and conditional execution stuff. I still would like to
know more about blocks.

Blocks come in three flavors: zero, one, or two arguments.

A *zero argument block* has no variables declared in
the block. Many of the conditional and iteration
messages in Smalltalk, including the Terminal
bell example shown earlier, use zero argument
blocks. For example:

```
x odd
   ifTrue: ['I"m odd']
   ifFalse: ['I"m even'].

[Time totalSeconds < 6480]
```

```
whileTrue: [
    Transcript show:
        'It is not time';
    cr].
Transcript show: 'It is time'.

| counter |
counter := 0.
[counter < 100] whileTrue: [
    counter := counter + 1.
    Terminal bell.]
```

Whoa, wait a microsecond!
What are the `whileTrue:`
and `whileFalse:` messages
about?

These are looping messages, which can be sent to
zero argument blocks. Both the `whileTrue:`
and `whileFalse:` messages iteratively execute
the code in their argument as long as the receiver
object returns the boolean they require to continue.

Simple, yes?

Yeah.

Another looping construct uses the `timesRe-`
`peat:` message and is implemented in the class
`Integer`. When sent to an integer it executes its
argument—a zero argument block—the integer
number of times. For example:

```
100 timesRepeat: [Terminal bell].
```

I was wondering how iteration would be implemented.
I'm glad we finally got to it.

There is more iteration to come, but for now let us
continue with the next flavor of block.

A *one argument block* takes one object as an argument. The variable used is declared at the front of the block. One argument blocks are used in some iteration statements.

The `to:do:` message lets you iterate over a range of numbers.

```
| array |
array := Array new: 20.
1 to: 20 do: [:index |
   array at: index
       put: index factorial].
| total |
total := 1.
1 to: 100 do: [:integer |
   total := total * integer].
```

The last time we met, you said you would tell me about some iteration messages for collections.

Yes, I did, and now is a good time.

Look in class `Collection`, and you will see the following iteration messages:

```
do:
collect:
select:
reject:
```

Each message takes a one argument block as an argument and executes the block for each element in the collection. The `collect:`, `select:`, and `reject:` messages also answer a new collection that is built based on the collection that received the message.

The `collect:` message maps the contents of the receiver collection to a collection of equal size.

Each element in the new collection is mapped, using the block, to the new collection. For example:

```
#(1 9 4) collect:
    [:num | num squared].
```

answers the collection #(1 81 16). Note that the elements in the collection have changed according to the code in the block.

The select: message picks particular elements from the receiver collection to put in another collection. The selection is done by the block. If it answers true, the element is added to the new collection; if it answers false, it is not. An example:

```
#(1 9 4 7) select:
    [:num | num > 5].
```

answers the collection #(9 7).

The reject: message works like select: but answers a collection of elements for which the block evaluates to false.

```
#(1 9 4 7) reject:
    [:num | num > 5].
```

answers the collection #(1 4).

This is more than I expected. Blocks are great!

Hold on, Jim. There is more.

A *two argument block* takes two objects as arguments. The variables used are declared at the front of the block. Two argument blocks are used for sort blocks and inject:into: messages.

The inject:into: message, which can be used to summarize the information in a collection, takes a starting point and a two argument block that combines elements as its arguments. The following statement, for example, sums all the numbers in the collection:

```
#(1 2 99 5)
   inject: 0
   into: [:sum :num | sum + num].
```

answers the number 107.

The `inject:into:` is not limited to adding numbers. For example:

```
#('I' 'like' 'Smalltalk')
   inject: (String new)
   into: [:sentence :word |
      sentence ,
         (String with: Space),
         word].
```

answers the string `'I like Smalltalk'`.

Wow! Blocks are really powerful.

Right (yawn . . .). Excuse me. Go back and implement the To Do List. I will get some rest. See you next time.

Summary

New Terms

Block	Iteration Message
Boolean	Comparison Message

What Have I Learned?

How to reference the boolean values true and false.

How to create booleans using comparison messages.

How to do conditional execution with ifTrue:ifFalse: messages.

How to use whileTrue: and other basic iteration messages.

How to iterate over collections in different ways.

Words of Wisdom

There is nothing magical about a block. It's an object and so can be assigned to variables, passed as arguments, and sent messages. You even can add new messages to its message interface. Here's an example of assigning a variable to a block:

```
| code |
code := [Terminal bell].
3 timesRepeat: code.
```

This may look strange, but it works fine.

If you don't like it, fix it. Most of Smalltalk is written in itself, with the source code available. This gives you wonderful flexibility, but makes it hard to complain.

To Do List

Blocks are implemented in the class Context and its subclasses. Spend some time looking at the message interface to these classes. Pay special attention to the value, value:, and value:value: methods. Also look at the message interface for the classes True and False. Look closely at the ifTrue:ifFalse: messages and how they are implemented.

Add the message ifNil: to the system. You should be able to send ifNil: to any object and have it answer itself if it isn't nil. If it is nil, then it should evaluate the argument (a block) with the value message and return that value. Here is an example of where this is useful (compare the uses of isNil and ifNil:):

```
^name isNil
    ifTrue: [String new]
    ifFalse: [name].
^name ifNil: [String new].
```

Hint: You will need to use, and to override, inheritance.

Use the disk browser to create a disk file with several lines of text. Open a workspace and write code that counts the number of each kind of character in the file (ignoring case). After you have the code working, add more code to print the results of the count onto the transcript window. The report should be in ASCII order.

The transcript window can be accessed by sending messages to the global variable Transcript. Some messages that the transcript can handle are nextPut:, nextPutAll:, and cr.

When writing the code, don't try to find the fastest or shortest code, instead go for the easiest to write.

8

OBJECT-ORIENTED THINKING AND DESIGN

Contents at: 'Chapter 8'

#(
Object-Oriented Thinking
    object-oriented thinking means thinking in objects
    object-oriented thinking tools
        metaphor
        visualization
        animation
        anthropomorphism
        perspective
Object-Oriented Design
    object-oriented design is prolonged object-oriented thinking
    assisted by a methodology
    focused on a particular goal
    An object-oriented design methodology:
        state the problem
        apply object-oriented thinking tools
        identify classes
        describe object states
        list message interfaces
        implement methods)

Questions of Interest

What is the object-oriented paradigm?
How can I make the shift?

Introduction

When you were first introduced to the object-oriented programming paradigm, you saw how to think of objects as computational entities and a bit about how to design software from objects and messages. In this chapter we will discuss in more detail the nature of the object-oriented paradigm.

The attention focused on the object-oriented paradigm usually centers around the objects that make up the implementation; little attention is paid to how the designer selects and creates the objects. While the object-oriented paradigm is about objects and messages, it is also about a new sort of problem solving, using objects as the fundamental unit of expression for the solution. This new way of problem solving requires a new mode of thinking and a new set of thinking tools. This shift is the essence of the object-oriented paradigm.

This chapter will introduce material that could make up another entire book. Use this now; you can learn more later.

Goals for this Chapter

To think about the real world in terms of objects and messages.

To find an effective path from the problem specification level to the object-oriented design level.

Jim   **Objective Wizard**

Hi! I'm back.

> Hello, Jim. How are your software development activities coming along?

Well, I understand the concepts, the language, and parts of the class hierarchy. I also can write code in Smalltalk. But I keep thinking in terms of data and structure. I have this recurring urge to construct a dataflow chart of my software. I also am having trouble designing software in this paradigm.

> Jim, look deep into my implementation. What do you see?

Variables, dataflow, control flow, and some other stuff.

> Jim, my procedural friend, you have not yet shifted your paradigm.

How can you tell?

> You still view software from the point of view of software abstractions (that is, data, control, and structure).

What? You mean after all our work I still don't understand this paradigm?

> I suspect you understand as much as you need, but

you are missing the knowledge and skill necessary
to apply what you understand.

So how should I view software in the object-oriented
paradigm?

When we write software in ObjectLand, we look to
the problem domain for descriptions of the solution. We design in terms of objects, state, and behavior as we see them in the problem domain. We
describe the elements of our software in the
domain vocabulary. We use the abstractions of the
ProblemWorld, not the abstractions of the software
domain.

Have you noticed that all software in the procedural
paradigm is expressed in terms of abstractions that
have meaning only within the computing world?

Yeah.

In ObjectLand we do not think in terms of Computer-
Land abstractions. Although we recognize that
there is a ComputerLand somewhere deep in each of
us, we also realize that there is a more expressive,
simple, and accurate way of describing the Problem-
World. That better way uses terms and abstractions
that actually exist in the ProblemWorld.

Sounds like I need a lesson in
object-oriented thinking.

Yes. The real shift in paradigm is the shift that
takes place in your mind. Object-Oriented Thinking is the essence of the object-oriented paradigm.

There are four essential components to the paradigm shift. You may find more, but you first need
to accept these before you can move on:

   1. Objects, messages, and methods are the
      building blocks of your solution.

2. Look to the problem for the solution and express the solution in the vocabulary of the problem domain.
3. Think in terms of modeling real world objects.
4. Apply a set of thinking tools to the ProblemWorld to create the SolutionWorld.

What do these thinking tools look like?

They are tools we use every day in the real world:

metaphor
visualization
animation
anthropomorphism
perspective

You will invent more as you grow as an object-oriented thinker.

All right, let's talk about metaphor.

A *metaphor* is an object that is like another object. Using a metaphor involves substituting one type of object in place of another to suggest or benefit from any likeness or analogy between them.

So what! How will metaphors help me design?

Think about it, Jim. In the object-oriented paradigm you actually are modeling a real world object or idea in ObjectLand. Your ability to create that model effectively is related to your knowledge of the real world object you are attempting to model. If you can create an intermediate object—a metaphorical object—in your design space, you have acquired more information about the real world object. You will have added your knowledge of the metaphorical object to your knowledge of the real world object you are trying to model.

By thinking in terms of metaphors of the problem you are trying to find, you will become a better solution finder.

How about an example?

OK. Imagine your application to be an object used to request information from somewhere on a computer network.

A metaphor might be one of those tear-off cards in magazines. Page through a magazine and rip out one of those cards. I will do the same.

What do you see on the card? What information does it request? How does it behave?

The one I am holding wants me to write my name and address, check off the information I want, and specify the form in which I want to receive the information. Then I should fold the card over, affix a stamp, and mail the card. If I accept this metaphor as reasonable for this application, which I do, then the information the object needs is:

> where to send the information,
> a list of information to get, and
> what form the information should take.

The behavior of the object should:

> pick the information needed, and
> transmit the request.

The "where to send the information" could be automated by using the magazine's address label or by writing in a different address.

Thinking of metaphors does seem to help create solutions. It almost seems that the metaphor itself is the solution.

Sometimes, yes. But usually the metaphor is an intermediate representation of the solution. A metaphor is a convenience when designing, and it also provides a good intermediate representation to which you can apply additional object-oriented thinking tools. For example, let us apply visualization to our metaphor object.

Wait. I want to know more about visualization before we attempt any integration with a metaphor.

Certainly. As a human you have a tremendous number of cortical neurons associated with visualization. As an object-oriented problem solver using visualization to examine a metaphorical object, you can bring much of your "wetware" online to give you additional insights into your solution space.

Sounds good, but how do I use it?

During daydreams you visualize something you enjoy. Daydreams are very visual, are they not?

Yes, they certainly are!

In ObjectLand what you call "daydreaming" we call *visualization* of objects of interest. The process is the same. If you can daydream, you can visualize. If you can visualize, you can "see" aspects of objects in much more detail and consequently implement them more completely.

Try it; it will make you a better object-oriented designer.

Wow, designing can be fun!
Give me an example.

> All right. Begin with a pen. Close your eyes and visualize the various characteristics of the pen. Then try to visualize the use of the pen.
>
> What do you see? What color and size is the nib? What is the pen doing?

So, visualizing my metaphorical object actually provides a
clearer understanding of the
solution?

> Very good! Notice that you are looking to the problem to find the solution. You are becoming an object-oriented thinker.

What's next?

> Try *animating* the object you are visualizing. Make the animated object behave how you want the Smalltalk object to behave. Keep in mind that the object you are animating is probably just a metaphor of the Smalltalk object you are design-ing. (Can you believe that some people actually can animate a Smalltalk object? I wonder what it looks like to them.)
>
> Animating your visualization is particularly helpful in modeling the behavior of the object you are de-signing. If you are having problems, try anthropo-morphism.

What's that?

> *Anthropomorphism* is the assignment of human or lifelike characteristics to an inanimate object. In this case you have an object in mind (literally) and assign it a personality (or at least some life-

like characteristics) to augment your visualization efforts.

It is helpful to think of personalities with which you are familiar. For example:

> manager
> mimic
> dispatcher
> agent

Actual people from the problem domain can be useful as animated objects (in your mind's eye, of course). When you use personalities from the problem domain you often envision a design that is close to implementation.

How about an example?

Sure. Other objects that get information include a messenger or even a dog who fetches a newspaper. The messenger is more capable, but the message interface to the dog is simpler.

Question: Which of the two "personalities" best fits your needs: the messenger or the dog?

Do you have more thinking tools?

Yes, many, but only one that I want to talk about right now.

What is it?

Perspective. As an object-oriented thinker you can make several important perspective changes, which may help in your design process. Try these three sometime:

Perspective One:

> Observe the object from a point outside the object.

Perspective Two:

> Observe the object from a point inside the object.

Perspective Three:

> Become the object and observe yourself.

Whew. I'm going to need an example.

> Let us use the tear-off response card example, viewing the visualized information card from three perspectives:

Perspective One:

> From outside the object, you tell it what information you need and where to send it. Then you tell it to do its stuff.

Perspective Two:

> From inside the object, you can watch what adding information does to your instance variables, any internal flags you might set, what to do if the user sends you off without filling in an address (that is, using a default address).

Perspective Three:

> By becoming the object, you access all your information and then go out and acquire the information. You are put into the mail, and you are delivered to where the information is kept.
>
> Now, do you return with the information, or

do you tell the recipient where and what to send?

What decisions are you making?

Are you confused?

Wiz, I don't think I'm in Kansas anymore.

What is a Kansas?

Never mind.

How can I put this all together?

Pick a problem of interest to you.

Now?

Yes!

OK. I'm ready.

Sit comfortably. Close your eyes and think about an object you have specified in your problem scope.

Ask yourself, "What object do I know about that is similar to this object?" (Metaphor)

When you find a suitable metaphor, visualize it in your mind's eye. Learn from what you see. (Visualization)

When you have a visualization, make it behave in some problem-domain way. Learn from your animation's behaviors. Watch the individual behaviors and the sequence in which they happen. (Animation)

Try assigning your object's responsibilities to a personality type. Run your animation with this personality substituted for your original metaphor. (Anthropomorphism)

Continue to watch your anthropomorphic animated visualization of a metaphorical object from your problem domain, then change your perspective. Move your mind's eye inside the visualization, perhaps to study a particular variable or characteristic. Become that variable or characteristic, noting how you change. (Perspective)

Wow! How can I learn to make this easier?

Practice. . . .

This is not programming as I learned it.

You are right; in fact, this is not programming at all.

It is a particular style of thinking/problem solving/analysis. Experiment with these techniques. They will make you a better object-oriented thinker and designer. In addition, these techniques fit in well with the basic design methodology we use in ObjectLand.

Thinking strategies such as these represent what is generally called "analysis" in other paradigms. As you can see, object-oriented design and development methodologies can be quite unconventional.

Methodologies?

Yes. As in all programming paradigms, there is a methodology to guide the innocent through the processes of analysis, design, and development.

What is the methodology you use?

I use a fundamental methodology that is simple but effective. I think you will like it.

I'm all ears.

In this methodology the completed design is never more than six steps away:

1. state the problem
2. visualize, et al.
3. objectify and classify
4. describe object states
5. describe the message interfaces
6. write the method code

While these steps appear sequential, they often are used in a rather "gestalt-based iteration," or in a style that attains the overall goal. Expect to iterate around in the methodology while you are working on the design.

I want to discuss these steps one at a time.

Let's go.

First state the problem. Your problem statement can take any form, as long as it is an effective way to describe the problem. Most people use a textual description initially, and then condense it into some form of graphical representation with circles, lines, etc. The statement should provide enough information about the problem so you can begin to design a solution. It also must state what the problem is not. The "problem is not" part of the description will provide a scope for the problem.

Any suggestions on how I can do this?

Sure. Use an erasable medium, such as a chalkboard, white board, or computer. Multiple drawing colors are useful.

Sit and think before writing anything down.

What's the next step?

Visualize the problem. If it is a window-based application, draw the window. Drawing continues your statement of the problem, and it is a big step in the iterative process of moving from problem to solution. In addition, visualizing will:

Help make the problem tangible.
Help bring out complexity.
Create a piece of the solution.
Provide an early focus on appearance.
Force a description of interactions.
Be done eventually anyway.

Any hints?

Yes. List any menu options. Pay attention to the relationships between windows and panes.

What is step three?

Identify objects in your visualization, and then group them into classes. This is the class definition step. You can do this on paper, but it is faster to do it in your mind. Think initially about your classes, and then use the class hierarchy browser to define them in your Smalltalk environment. Designing your classes in the class hierarchy browser allows you to begin developing concurrently with your initial design process.

I've got the classes. Now what do I do with them?

In step four you describe the information contained

in your classes. The information contained in your objects will be defined in the objects' class and instance variables. The information each object has to maintain can be identified by thinking about the behavior of the object.

At this point, if you are having trouble determining what information your object should contain, use some object-oriented thinking tools. For example, change perspective.

You might as well enter your class definitions using the class hierarchy browser now.

Hints?

Do not worry about getting it right the first time.

Are we done yet?

Not yet. List the message interfaces for each of your classes. Since objects only interface to the real world through their message interfaces, this step will largely determine the behavior of your objects. Use the menus from the window drawing in step two. Each menu option is an action and should be reflected in the message interface.

When you are dealing with a large number of messages (more than 10), list them in functional groups that reflect facets of the object's behavior.

What is step six?

Write the methods to implement each message. Up till now you have written little code (class definition is code writing). Step six is code writing in a more conventional sense. When you are done, you will have completed the first pass on your project. It will behave as you designed it, and it will be ready to show you how it works. Next you iterate over the steps in the methodology to improve your design. Do this until you are satisfied.

I'd like to try this methodology out.

> Sure. The To Do List has some ideas. But before
> you go, Jim, look deep into my implementation.
> What do you see now?

My gawd! You're full of objects!

> Jim, you have made the paradigm shift.

Summary

New Terms

Metaphor   Visualization

Animation   Anthropomorphism

Perspective   Methodology

Iterative Design and Development

What Have I Learned?

Some differences between conventional analysis and object-oriented thinking.

Some general thinking tools that can be useful in object-oriented thinking, including metaphor, visualization, animation, and perspective.

A simple six-step object-oriented design and development methodology.

Words of Wisdom

Define your problem.

Problem definition may not be half the battle, but it does keep you from wasting your time solving a problem that doesn't need to be solved.

Defining what your problem isn't is at least as important as defining what your problem is.

When you begin to design a solution, keep things as changeable as possible. The more you design, the more you will understand the problem, which will enable you to modify your design some more. This loop is more productive if it is easy to change the design.

It is easiest to make changes in your head; writing things down makes them much harder to change.

To Do List

With the design and development methodology presented in this chapter, a first pass design can be done very quickly. Design three of the following, taking no more than a half hour each (fifteen minutes is better):

1. An appointment book.
2. A control system for an automated donut factory.
3. An inventory system for a collector (stamp, coin, car).
4. An investment tracking system.

When you finish, evaluate your performance, asking yourself:

1. How much time did I take for each design?
2. Did I get faster on the latter designs?
3. What recording mediums did I use (paper, white board, computer, etc.)?
4. Did I complete all steps for each problem?

Design your current project or a part that's small enough to move through steps one through five in an hour. If it takes less than an hour, good.

Take one of the first pass designs from above and refine the design. Don't spend more than an hour. Try to get to where you are actually writing code for some of the messages in your object's message interface.

Try experimenting with different ways of doing designs. For example, do as much of the design in your head as you can before writing things down. The more you can do in this fashion, the faster the problem is solved. With practice, you may work through the first four or five design iterations without writing down more than a few notes.

When you write down your design, use an easily changeable medium. In Object-Land, we prefer a large white board with several colored markers. If possible, try doing a tandem design with a coworker. This takes longer, but the designs are more robust.

9

A TASTE OF THE FUTURE

Questions of Interest

> What can I do now?
> Where do I go from here?
> How do I get there?

Introduction

If you are here, either you are one of those people who reads the end first or you have finished the first nine chapters. If you have read the rest, I am confident that you have learned what you set out to learn. But you are probably asking, "Is this all there is?"

Well, no. There is much, much more. You are now a beginner. This chapter tells you how to become more expert.

You probably will need more information (a reference list from the ObjectLand database is included at the end of the book).

You also should begin immediately to think in terms of objects and to write code in Smalltalk. You are ready now. Don't wait.

Goals for this Chapter

> To understand what you have learned.
> To know what you have yet to learn.
> To identify strategies for learning the rest.
> To be motivated to write Smalltalk code.

Jim   **Objective Wizard**

I can't believe I'm to the last
chapter!

> Yes, you have completed your training. You are
> now what we in ObjectLand call an OOH (Object-
> Oriented Human).

It's difficult to see what I've
accomplished in this short
time.

> Well, you have a new way of viewing problem
> solving (the object-oriented paradigm), a new set
> of implementation tools (objects, messages, meth-
> ods, classes, instances, encapsulation, polymor-
> phism, and inheritance), and a new programming
> language (Smalltalk) with which to express object-
> oriented solutions.
>
> You also have written a small amount of
> Smalltalk/V code.
>
> I am impressed. How about you?

When you put it that way. I
accomplished more than I
thought, and it was fun (most
of the time).

Where do I go from here?

> Let us start with the paradigm.

What about the paradigm?

> As you now know, a *paradigm* is a perspective
> of viewing an activity or a phenomenon. With the
> object-oriented paradigm, the activity is a particu-

lar domain of problem solving called "computer programming."

To take advantage of this paradigm:

1. Be aware of it.
2. Understand it. Your understanding of the object-oriented paradigm is incomplete at this time. You must spend more time in ObjectLand, and you also must read some of the books from the ObjectLand library.
3. Use it. Apply it to your everyday world. During our brief discussion on the nature of object-oriented thinking, I gave you an object-oriented thinking toolbox. We talked about how you could use these tools to facilitate software design. In reality (reality?), these tools can be applied to any problem, not just software problems. As you think your way through your everyday world, use object-oriented thinking as often as you can. Have fun with it. The more you use it, the more skillful you will become.

What about application building? I need to build window-based applications, but I still don't know how. What am I going to do?

Building window-based applications is not a simple task, but I suspect that you know more than you realize.

During the lesson on object-oriented design, we discussed a methodology that works well for designing window-based applications. You have a number of examples already implemented for you in the Smalltalk programming interface. Model your application after them. Use and modify the code in them. You will learn a lot about window-based applications by working with the examples provided.

You can read and write Smalltalk code.

You also can return to ObjectLand for further enlightenment.

That's not much help to me now.

Jim, you have come a long way in a short time. Window-based applications are complex to implement. You will need some time to master them.

The future holds interesting alternatives to the conventional implementation strategies for window-based applications. There are several organizations in ObjectLand that have implemented tools to make window design and development much, much, much easier. These tools will be a big help to you.

How about some help now?

Jim, you sound impatient, but I understand your need. I have included a recipe for a small, window-based application called `SalesMonitor` in your To Do List for this chapter. Read it fully and slowly. Read all the code, as you learned in Chapter 2, while you type it in. Reading the code will help you understand. If a particular message send confuses you, look at the class of the object receiving the message and use the class hierarchy browser to get more information.

The sequence of the code presented in the `Sales-Monitor` recipe is the recommended sequence for writing code for a window-based application.

Consider it a gift from ObjectLand.

Thank you!

What are some of the advanced programming ideas I can use to benefit from the object-oriented paradigm?

Here are a few that might tickle your memory chips:

encapsulators
mimics
teammates
managers
rovers

Let us talk about them one at a time.

OK. Encapsulators first.

An *encapsulator* is an object that contains other objects, essentially adding specialized functions. Encapsulators protect the objects they contain from inappropriate usage by other objects. They also can act as message filters, limiting the messages that can get to the contained object.

How about an example?

The `Stack` class you implemented in Chapter 6 is an encapsulator. It contains a collection but constrains it to behave like a stack.

What are mimics?

Mimics, objects that use polymorphism extensively, have message interfaces similar to the object they mimic. Examples can be found in the `Magnitude` and `Collection` hierarchies. The example I used to illustrate the polymorphic characteristics of the + message demonstrated the mimiclike behavior of the `Number` subclasses.

What do teammates do?

Teammates are classes of objects specifically designed to work with other classes to do some task. The Model-Pane-Dispatcher application-building strategy found in Smalltalk/V, V286, and VMac is an excellent example of teamwork. In this case the task is application building.

I think I can guess what managers do.

Good. What do you think?

Managers are objects that manage other objects, probably by controlling access to the objects that they manage.

Right! Very good.

At an implementation level, controlling access might mean managing the message passing between the objects being managed. An example might be a spreadsheet manager who manages the cells in the spreadsheet.

Managers were intuitive for me. What is a rover?

A *rover* moves across collections of objects, manipulating them in some consistent manner. A simulation represents an opportunity for a rover to update all objects involved in the simulation.

In all these ideas, you are thinking anthropomorphically about the objects that you are implementing. Isn't that correct?

Yes, that is true. Personifying the objects you are

implementing helps to make more powerful objects. The ideas in this chapter represent implementation-level thinking about the notion of intelligent, interacting objects that behave like people.

These are really exciting. Let's begin working with them!

No, Jim. This journey to ObjectLand is complete. You have learned what you came here to learn, and now you have to get back to work. You now understand the paradigm and enough of the Smalltalk language to begin solving problems.

Go forth and write code.

But I want to learn this future stuff.

Use what you have learned and come back in the future to learn the "future stuff."

How will I learn these skills of my programming future?

When you are ready to learn them, I will be ready to teach them. When you are ready, look for other ObjectLand books.

Yum!

Poached paradigm in a Bag.

Why, Jim, I believe you have acquired an object-oriented sense of humor. Hope to see you again.

It has been fun!

To Do List

Most of your future Smalltalk programming will involve implementing window-based applications. Window-based applications can be complex, so you will need time to learn how to put one together. In ObjectLand we ask beginners to build their first applications from recipes.

An ObjectLand application recipe provides all the ingredients necessary to implement an application. It also tells how much of what to put where and when. When you bake bread, for example, you don't want to be bothered with biochemistry of what's happening. You don't want to grow the flour or refine the sugar. You just want to bake bread, it's the bread that counts. You expect to use preexisting components to implement the bread. An ObjectLand recipe is similar. We provide the components and the instructions for combining them, and then you make the application. Try it. It's an excellent first step to application building.

This recipe works best when read in front of a Smalltalk/V system. As you read, you will come across pieces of code; enter and save these before you move on. You are not simply a sophisticated input device, however. Read the code as you enter it; try to understand what is happening. When you reach the end, you will, short of any typos, have a working application you can examine and enhance. A list of possible enhancements is included at the end of the text.

Let us build a simple sales monitor, which we can use to enter and track sales in a record store or similar establishment.

Applications can be broken down into two parts: the representation and the user interface. The *representation* is a bunch of data and behavior that represents the problem. In our case the representation must be able to store the kind and number of products sold and add new items and sales. To save time, trouble, and trees we will keep the representation simple. The *user interface* consists of the windows, menus, buttons, and other user-manipulable items on the screen. Most of window-based application building deals with building the user interface.

We'll start with the representation. To help keep things simple, let us represent products to be sold as strings. For example, a compact disc might be represented as the name of its artist; thus the CD "A1A" would be represented by 'Jimmy Buffett'.

Now we need a way to keep track of sales. Open a class hierarchy browser and add the class SalesRecorder as a subclass of Object so the class definition looks like:

```
Object subclass: #SalesRecorder
    instanceVariableNames:
        'productSales'
    classVariableNames: ''
    poolDictionaries: ''
```

This class tracks how many of each product we've sold. We make the instance variable `productSales` a dictionary, where each product is a key and the related value is the number sold. Since `productSales` must be initialized to a dictionary, we override the class message `new` and create a matching `initialize` instance message:

```
new                    (class message)
    "Answer an initialized instance."
^super new initialize

initialize             (instance message)
    "Private - Initialize my instance variables."
productSales := Dictionary new.
```

These two messages ensure that our instance variable is initialized to an empty dictionary as soon as the instance of `SalesRecorder` is created.

Now we add messages that let us add products, record sales of products, and query the current sales information. Let's start with the method `addProduct:`, which takes a string as an argument (remember we are representing products as strings) and adds it to the products whose sales are being tracked.

```
addProduct: aProduct
    "Add a new product to the sales record."
(productSales includesKey: aProduct)
    ifFalse: [productSales at: aProduct put: 0].
```

Note that we initialize the products sales number to zero, which seems reasonable. We also do nothing if the product already exists. This keeps us from accidentally resetting sales to zero on an already existing product.

Once we've added a product, we want to record its sales. Let us assume we sell only one, or at least a small number, of a given product at a time. As a result, we can add sales by using an `addSale:` message, where the argument is a string that represents a product we've already added.

```
addSale: aProduct
    "Increment the sales counter for aProduct."
self checkProduct: aProduct.
productSales
at: aProduct
put: (productSales at: aProduct) + 1.
```

Here we simply incremented the number of sales for the given product. The message `checkProduct:` is a private message that signals an error if the product is not one we are tracking.

```
checkProduct: aProduct
   "Private - Signal an error if aProduct is not one
   of the products whose sales I am tracking."
(productSales includesKey: aProduct)
   ifFalse: [^self error: 'Unknown product ', aProduct].
```

Now we need to add some methods that let us get at sales information. One method is `products`, which answers a collection of all the products we are tracking. Another is `numberSoldOf:`, which answers how many of a particular product have been sold.

```
products
   "Answer collection of the products I track."
^productSales keys.

numberSoldOf: aProduct
   "Answer the number of sales for aProduct."
self checkProduct: aProduct.
^productSales at: aProduct.
```

That's all we need to do before building our window-based interface. There is, of course, much more we could do. A `removeSale:` message, which decrements the number sold for a particular product, would be nice, just in case we make a mistake or get a product returned. We also could be more relaxed and change `checkProduct:` so it adds a product if it doesn't find it (instead of signaling an error).

A more complete overhaul that included classes like `Product`, `Sale`, and `SalesReturn` would be necessary if we put this application into production. Spend some time thinking about how you would improve this representation, but wait until you've done the next part of the recipe. It's sure to give you ideas.

Oh, one more thing. In a workspace, type in and execute:

```
Sales := SalesRecorder new.
Sales addProduct: 'Madonna'.
Sales addProduct: 'Jimmy Buffett'.
Sales addSale: 'Madonna'.
```

We have added two products and recorded one sale—the first sale in our newly opened used CD store!

The remainder of this recipe is separated into two implementations: one for Smalltalk/VDOS, V286, and VMac; the other for Smalltalk/VPM and VWindows. Go to the recipe for your version of Smalltalk.

Good luck!

SalesMonitor Recipe for Smalltalk/VDOS, V286, and VMac

Window-based applications are created by a cooperative effort between three kinds of objects: panes, dispatchers, and models. Panes display information to the user; dispatchers handle user input from the mouse and keyboard; and models control the application. Since Smalltalk already includes a good selection of panes and dispatchers, the real work involves designing and creating the model. This application-building strategy is called Model-Pane-Dispatcher (MPD).

You can see a complete list of the available subpanes by using a class hierarchy browser to look at the subclasses of `SubPane`. Since we will display a single list of products, we will use just one list pane.

Every window needs a special pane, a *top pane*, to manage the subpanes and provide the functionality associated with the entire window. These panes are instances of `TopPane`.

The Interface

We will keep our user interface as simple as possible, with just one window containing one pane and one short menu. The pane will contain a list of the products sold and how many of each were sold. We will leave enhancements—such as showing the total number sold or showing more information on each product—for later.

Since we plan to display a list of products, we will use a list pane. Our menu needs only two options: one to add a sale and one to create a new product. You may find it useful to sketch the window and its associated menu.

So far we've created our representation (an instance of `SalesRecorder` in the global variable `Sales`), picked the panes to be in our window (a single list pane), and chosen our menu options (Add Product and Make a Sale). The only thing left is to create the model.

Create the Model Class

First create the model class and give it appropriate instance variables. Always create an instance variable for each pane in the window; this makes it easier for the model to interact with the panes. Most applications have other instance variables to keep track of the state of the application, and ours is no exception. We will use one variable to access the instance of `SalesRecorder`, one to hold a sorted list of all the products we sell, and another to keep track of the currently selected product.

To create the model class, select the class `Object` and create a subclass called `SalesMonitor`. Now add the instance variables so the class definition looks like:

```
Object subclass: #SalesMonitor
    instanceVariableNames:
        'listPane salesRecorder productList selected'
    classVariableNames: ' '
    poolDictionaries: ' '
```

Save the changes to the class definition.

The Open Method

The `open` or `openOn:` method, used to activate the application, has four responsibilities:

1. initialize the application
2. create the panes
3. add the subpanes to the top pane
4. open the application window

Here is the `open` method for `SalesMonitor`:

```
open
    "Open the sales monitor application window."
| topPane |
self initializeApplication.
topPane := self makeTopPane.
listPane := self makeListPane.
topPane addSubpane: listPane.
topPane dispatcher open scheduleWindow.
```

Note that there is one private method to create each pane. The last statement, which tells the windowing system to open the application window, may look a little strange. Treat it as something the system takes care of for you. Don't worry about what it is doing.

We would use an `openOn:` method if we wanted to pass some information to the application. For example, we could have passed the object acting as the sales recorder instead of using the global variable `Sales`.

Initializing the Application

Initialization usually consists of initializing instance variables that keep track of internal application information. For the sales monitor we will build a list of all the products in the global variable `Sales`, making sure that the currently selected item is set to none (`nil`).

```
initializeApplication
    "Private - Initialize the applications instance
variables."
salesRecorder := Sales.
productList := salesRecorder products asSortedCollection.
selected := nil.
```

Creating the Panes

We use methods called "make methods" to create our panes. A *make method* creates, initializes, and answers a pane. This reduces the size of our open method and makes it easy to steal code for another application. Here are the make methods for the sales monitor:

```
makeTopPane
    "Private - Create and answer a new top pane."
^TopPane new
    label: 'Sales Monitor';
    yourself.

makeListPane
    "Private - Create and answer a list pane to display
    the current sales situation."
^ListPane new
    model: self;
    name: #displayList;
    change: #select:;
    menu: #salesMenu;
    returnIndex: true;
    framingRatio: (0@0 corner: 1@1);
    yourself.
```

The `makeTopPane` method creates an instance of `TopPane`, sets its label, and answers the new top pane. The `makeListPane` method is more complicated than `makeTopPane`, but you can treat the `model:`, `returnIndex:`, and `yourself` as fixed. The `name:` message specifies a message sent to the model when the pane needs a new list to display. The `change:` method specifies a message sent when the user picks an item from the list. Similarly, `menu:` specifies a message sent to the model when the pane needs to pop up a menu. Some use the `returnIndex:` message with list panes, preferring to deal with indexes rather than the strings that the list pane displays.

The `framingRatio:` message specifies what portion of the window this pane uses. This sounds and is simple, provided you have only a few panes and each takes a fixed ratio of the window's space. To see a more complex use of `framing-Ratio:` (and its nasty brother `framingBlock:`), look at the `openOn:` method in `ClassHierarchyBrowser`.

The Name and Change Methods

Name methods deal with the information displayed in the pane. List panes expect an indexed collection of one-line strings. Here's the name method for our list pane:

```
displayList
    "Private - List pane name handler.
     Answer a list of all the products followed by the
     number sold of each."
^productList collect: [:product |
    product ,
        (String with: $, with: $ ) ,
        (salesRecorder numberSoldOf: product)
            printString].
```

Here we're building a list of product names and tacking on the number sold. To do this we use the product list we built when we initialized the application, and then we make a new list by concatenating on the number sold for each product. Notice that we are answering a list of strings. That's what list panes like to see.

Change methods handle change to the pane caused by user input. For list panes this means the user selected an item in the list. The pane automatically highlights the selected line. We just have to know about the selection and handle any side effects.

```
select: anIndex
    "Private - List pane change handler.
     The user picked an item from the list pane. Track
     the item."
selected := productList at: anIndex.
```

Since there aren't any side effects, we just have to worry about keeping track of the selected item. If you're wondering what a side effect is, see what happens to the text pane on the bottom of a class hierarchy browser when you select a method. That's a side effect.

Menus

When we created the list pane in the `makeListPane` method, we specified a menu message name with `menu: #salesMenu;`. Menu messages, like name and change messages, are implemented as methods in the model. Menu messages answer a menu (an instance of `Menu`), which is picked up and used by the windowing system.

Here's the code for the Smalltalk/VDOS and V286 versions:

```
salesMenu
    "Private - List pane menu handler.
     Answer a menu for the list pane."
^Menu
    labelArray: #('Add Product' 'Make Sale')
    lines: #()
    selectors: #(addProduct makeSale)
```

We need a slightly different version for Smalltalk/VMac. Because the Macintosh windowing system has a menu bar, the menus need titles:

```
salesMenu
    "Private - List pane menu handler.
     Answer a menu for the list pane."
^ (Menu
    labelArray: #('Add Product' 'Make Sale')
        lines: #()
        selectors: #(addProduct makeSale))
    title: 'Sales';
    yourself
```

This menu has two options, as we specified earlier. The code to implement these options needs to be implemented in the methods `addProduct` and `makeSale` in our model.

The menu option method `addProduct` prompts the user for a new product name and adds it to our sales tracking object. We also need to update the list pane with the new information and make sure the item highlighted in the list pane is the one we just added.

```
addProduct
    "Private - Menu option handler.
     Prompt the user for a new product and add the
     product to the sales recorder."
| newProduct |
newProduct := self getNewProduct.
newProduct isNil ifFalse: [
    salesRecorder addProduct: newProduct.
    productList :=
        salesRecorder products asSortedCollection.
    listPane restoreSelected:
        (productList indexOf: newProduct).
    selected := newProduct].
```

Take a minute and see if you can match what this method needs to do with the lines
of code that do it. Note that the message getNewProduct gets the name of the
product from the user.

```
getNewProduct
    "Private - Get a new product name from the user.
     Answer the name if it is valid, and nil otherwise."
| answer |
answer := Prompter
    prompt: 'Enter the new product name:'
    default: ''.
^(answer isNil or: [productList includes: answer])
    ifTrue: [nil]
    ifFalse: [answer].
```

The getNewProduct method helps reduce the complexity of addProduct,
which was getting too large to be readable.

The menu option method makeSale should add a sale to the currently selected
product. It also should make certain the pane is updated with the new information.

```
makeSale
    "Private - Menu option handler.
     Add a sale to the selected product."
selected isNil ifFalse: [
    salesRecorder addSale: selected.
    listPane restoreSelected: (productList indexOf:
        selected)].
```

The End?

That's it. If you've been typing this in as you went along, you can start it now by typing the following in a workspace or in the system transcript and executing it with a "do it":

```
SalesMonitor new open.
```

If you want to make enhancements, I have a few suggestions.

Add a new menu option called "Remove Product" to eliminate products you no longer carry. You also could add a "Remove Sale" option to delete a single sale (in case a customer returns something).

The number sold is difficult to read because it is always listed right after the product's name. Try to find a way to make these elements line up in a column. You may want to look into the subclasses of `Stream` and the `String` method `asStream`.

Maintain more information about each product, including price, cost, and number available for sale.

Allow the use of multiple sale recorders. In other words, stop using a global variable to store your sales recorder.

Create a sales report. Print it onto the transcript window if you don't have a printer.

Track sales by the day.

There are many more possibilities. Try to have fun while learning about creating window-based applications in Smalltalk.

Happy Smalltalking!

SalesMonitor Recipe for Smalltalk/VPM and VWindows

Window-based applications are created by a cooperative effort between two kinds of objects: view managers and subpanes. View managers control the application and window, while subpanes display information to the user. Since Smalltalk already includes a good selection of subpanes, the real work involves designing and creating the view manager. Fortunately much of the work is done for us. After we make our view manager a subclass of `ViewManager`, we inherit much of the window and user-input control capabilities.

You can see a complete list of the available subpanes by using a class hierarchy browser to look at the the subclasses of `SubPane`. Since we will display a single list of products, we will use just one list pane.

The Interface

We will keep our user interface as simple as possible, with just one window containing one pane and one short menu. The pane will contain a list of the products sold and how many of each were sold. We will leave enhancements—such as showing the total number sold or showing more information on each product—for later.

Since we plan to display a list of products, we will use a list pane. Our menu needs only two options: one to add a sale and one to create a new product. You may find it useful to sketch the window and its associated menu.

So far we've created our representation (an instance of `SalesRecorder` in the global variable `Sales`), picked the panes to be in our window (a single list pane), and chosen our menu options (Add Product and Make a Sale). The only thing left is to create the view manager.

Create the View Manager Class

First create the view manager class and give it appropriate instance variables. Always create an instance variable for each pane in the window; this makes it easier for the view manager to interact with the panes. Most view managers have other instance variables to keep track of the state of the application, and ours is no exception. We will use one variable to access the instance of `SalesRecorder`, one to hold a sorted list of all the products we sell, and another to keep track of the currently selected product.

To create the view manager class, select the class `ViewManager`, and create a subclass called `SalesMonitor`. Now add instance variables so the class definition looks like:

```
ViewManager subclass: #SalesMonitor
instanceVariableNames:
   'listPane salesRecorder productList selected '
   classVariableNames: ''
   poolDictionaries: ''
```

Save the changes to the class definition.

The Open Method

The `open` or `openOn:` method, used to activate the application, has four responsibilities:

1. initialize the application
2. create the panes
3. add the subpanes to the view manager
4. open the application window

Here is the `open` method for `SalesMonitor`:

```
open
    "Open the sales monitor application window."
self initializeApplication.
self label: 'Sales Monitor'.
listPane := self makeListPane.
self addSubpane: listPane.
self openWindow.
```

Note that we used a private method to create the subpane.

We would use an `openOn:` method if we wanted to pass some information to the application. For example, we could have passed the object acting as the sales recorder instead of using the global variable `Sales`.

Initializing the Application

Initialization usually consists of initializing instance variables that keep track of internal application information. For the sales monitor we will build a list of all the products in the global variable `Sales`, making sure that the currently selected item is set to none (`nil`).

```
initializeApplication
    "Private - Initialize the applications instance
    variables."
salesRecorder := Sales.
productList := salesRecorder products asSortedCollection.
selected := nil.
```

Creating the Pane

We use a method called a "make method" to create our pane. A *make method* creates, initializes, and answers a pane. This reduces the size of our `open` method and makes it easy to steal code for another application. Here is the make method for the sales monitor:

```
makeListPane
    "Private - Create and answer a new list pane."
```

```
^ListPane new
    owner: self;
    when: #getContents perform: #displayList:;
    when: #select perform: #select:;
    when: #getMenu perform: #salesMenu:;
    framingRatio: (0@0 corner: 1@1);
    yourself.
```

The `makeListPane` method is fairly complicated, but you can treat the `owner:` and `yourself` messages as fixed. The `when:perform:` messages specify a message sent to the view manager when a particular event occurs. Here `#getContents` happens when the pane needs information to display, and `#select` happens when the user selects an item from a list pane. Similarly, `#getMenu:` is sent when the pane needs a menu.

The `framingRatio:` message specifies what portion of the window this pane uses. This sounds and is simple, provided you have only a few panes and each takes a fixed ratio of the window's space. To see a more complex use of `framingRatio:` (and its nasty brother `framingBlock:`), look at the `openOn:` method in `ClassHierarchyBrowser`.

Event Handling Methods

Methods that handle the `#getContents` event set the contents of the pane to whatever that pane needs to display. List panes expect an indexed collection of one-line strings. Here's the `#getContents` handler for our list pane:

```
displayList: aPane
    "Private - List pane getContents event handler.
    Set the contents of the list pane to a list of
    all the products followed by the number sold
    of each."
aPane contents:
    (productList collect: [:product |
        product ,
        (String with: $, with: $ ) ,
            (salesRecorder numberSoldOf: product)
                printString]).
```

Here we're setting the pane contents to a list of product names and tacking on the number sold. To do this we use the product list we built when we initialized the application, and then we make a new list by concatenating on the number sold for each product. Notice that we set the contents to a list of strings. That's what list panes like to see.

The handler for the #select event handles the user selecting one of the items in the list. The pane automatically highlights the selected line. We just have to know about the selection and handle any side effects.

```
select: aPane
    "Private - List pane select handler.
     The user picked an item from the list pane.
     Track the item."
selected := productList at: aPane selection.
```

Since there aren't any side effects, we just have to worry about keeping track of the selected item. If you're wondering what a side effect is, see what happens to the text pane on the bottom of a class hierarchy browser when you select a method. That's a side effect.

Menus

When we created the list pane in the makeListPane method, we specified a #getMenu event handler. The #getMenu handler sets the menu for the pane to an instance of Menu, which is put on the windows action bar and used as a pop-up menu for the associated pane.

```
salesMenu: aPane
    "Private - List pane getMenu event handler.
     Set the menu for the list pane."
aPane setMenu:
    (Menu new
        appendItem: 'Add &Product' selector: #addProduct;
        appendItem: 'Make &Sale' selector: #makeSale;
        title: '&Sales';
        owner: self;
        yourself).
```

This menu has two options, as we specified earlier. The code to implement those options needs to be implemented in the methods addProduct and makeSale in our view manager.

The ampersands (&) precede the character used to access the menu via the keyboard. If you are using VPM, replace & with ~.

The menu option method addProduct prompts the user for a new product name and adds it to our sales tracking object. We also need to update the list pane with the new information and make sure the item highlighted in the list pane is the one we just added.

```
addProduct
    "Private - Menu option handler.
     Prompt the user for a new product and add
     the product to the sales recorder."
| newProduct |
newProduct := self getNewProduct.
newProduct isNil ifFalse: [
    salesRecorder addProduct: newProduct.
    productList :=
        salesRecorder products asSortedCollection.
    listPane restoreSelected:
        (productList indexOf: newProduct).
    selected := newProduct].
```

Take a minute and see if you can match what this method needs to do with the lines of code that do it. Note that the message getNewProduct gets the name of the product from the user.

```
getNewProduct
    "Private - Get a new product name from the user.
     Answer the name if it is valid, and nil otherwise."
| answer |
answer := Prompter
    prompt: 'Enter the new product name:'
    default: ''.
^(answer isNil or: [productList includes: answer])
    ifTrue: [nil]
    ifFalse: [answer].
```

The getNewProduct method helps reduce the complexity of addProduct, which was getting too large to be readable.

The menu option method makeSale should add a sale to the currently selected product. It also should make certain the pane is updated with the new information.

```
makeSale
    "Private - Menu option handler.
     Add a sale to the selected product."
selected isNil ifFalse: [
    salesRecorder addSale: selected.
    listPane restoreSelected:
        (productList indexOf: selected)].
```

The End?

That's it. If you've been typing this in as you went along, you can start it now by typing the following in a workspace or in the system transcript and executing it with a "do it":

```
SalesMonitor new open.
```

If you want to make enhancements, I have a few suggestions.

Add a new menu option called "Remove Product" to eliminate products you no longer carry. You also could add a "Remove Sale" option to remove a single sale (in case a customer returns something).

The number sold is difficult to read because it is always listed right after the product's name. Try to find a way to make these elements line up in a column. You may want to look into the subclasses of `Stream` and the `String` method `asStream`. I also suggest you use a monospaced font.

Maintain more information about each product, including price, cost, and number available for sale.

Allow the use of multiple sale recorders. In other words, stop using a global variable to store your sales recorder.

Create a sales report. Print it onto the transcript window if you don't have a printer.

Track sales by the day.

There are many more possibilities. Try to have fun while learning about creating window-based applications in Smalltalk.

Happy Smalltalking!

GLOSSARY

ACTIVATE. *See* METHOD ACTIVATION.

ANALOGY. A thinking tool useful in object-oriented thinking and design. The comparison of an understood framework to one less well understood in the hope of transferring knowledge about the first to the second. *See also* OBJECT-ORIENTED THINKING and METAPHOR.

ANIMATION. A thinking tool useful in object-oriented thinking and design. The imaginary visualization of an object's behavior (visualizing the behavior often brings out hidden complexities). *See also* OBJECT-ORIENTED THINKING and VISUALIZATION.

ANSWER. *See* RETURN.

ANTHROPOMORPHISM. A thinking tool useful in object-oriented thinking and design. The assigning of human personality characteristics to virtual objects; some common personality types are managers, teammates, and rovers. *See also* OBJECT-ORIENTED THINKING.

APPLICATION. A solution to some problem expressed in Smalltalk (or some other programming system). Consists of one or more windows that provide a user interface and some objects that represent the information and behavior of real world objects in the solution. *See also* ITERATIVE REFINEMENT, WINDOW, and METHODOLOGY.

ARGUMENT. An object passed to a method as part of a message send. Binary and keyword messages always have arguments; unary messages never do. Blocks also can be passed arguments.

ASSIGNMENT. The operation changing the object that a variable references. Done using the colon-equal (: =) operator. It is not a binary message send. *See also* VARIABLE.

BINARY MESSAGE. A message with exactly one argument. Normally used for messages that do arithmetic or compare two objects. Binary messages consists of one or two special characters. *See also* MESSAGE and ORDER OF EXECUTION.

BLACKY. A large, black, four-footed entity existing in the RealWorld. Although he looks like a dog, his IQ is estimated to be 402. We have no explanation, but our current hypothesis has to do with time travel, advanced five-dimensional processing systems, and superconducting drool. *See also* GARBAGE COLLECTOR.

BLOCK. A piece of code packaged as an object. Implemented as instances of `Context` or one of its subclasses. Defined by surrounding a piece of code with brackets (`[ ]`). Blocks can have zero, one, or two arguments.

CLASS. A template for creating objects. All objects are instances of a class; classes define the behavior for their instances and what instance variables they will have, but not the value of the instance variables. *See also* CLASS VARIABLE, CLASS METHOD, INSTANCE, and INHERITANCE.

CLASS VARIABLE. A variable associated with a class, accessible by the class's methods and instances. Also accessible to the classes subclasses and their instances. Class variables always start with a capital letter. *See also* VARIABLE, POOL VARIABLE, INSTANCE VARIABLE, and GLOBAL VARIABLE.

COMPUTERLAND. The normal Von Neumann-style computer. Also, systems that are created (programmed) in a procedural fashion, since the procedural paradigm is close to the hardware.

DO IT. A menu option that compiles and executes selected code in a text pane. Also, the action of selecting a piece of code and executing it with this menu option. *See also* SHOW IT.

DYNAMIC BINDING. Capability of some object-oriented systems to choose the code to be executed when a particular message is sent at run time. Also called late binding. *See also* POLYMORPHISM, MESSAGE, and METHOD.

ENCAPSULATION. The protection and containment of variables and methods. Objects have a private inside, consisting of variables and methods, and a public outside, consisting of a message interface. You can access an object only by sending it a message. *See also* MESSAGE and MESSAGE INTERFACE.

EXPRESSION. *See* STATEMENT.

GARBAGE COLLECTOR. The part of the Smalltalk run-time system that looks for unused objects and reclaims the memory they are using. It keeps us from having to worry about deallocating objects with which we are done. Creating (and understanding) garbage collectors is an arcane art best left to those brilliant and slightly insane people who enjoy such things. *See also* BLACKY.

IMPLEMENTORS. Methods that implement a particular message, as in "the implementors of the `at:put:` message." Also, the option on the methods menu in the class hierarchy browser that creates a list of the implementors of a message. *See also* SENDERS.

INHERITANCE. When a class is given the state and behavior of its superclass, which it can then add to or modify to define a new class. Classes inherit instance and class methods, class variables, and instance variable templates from their superclasses. *See also* SUPERCLASS and SUBCLASS.

INSTANCE. An object that is not a class. Also, any object that has some particular class, as in "The variable A contains an instance of `Array`." *See also* CLASS and OBJECT.

INSTANCE VARIABLE. A variable associated with an instance. Accessible by the instance methods of the instance's class and by the instance methods of its subclasses. Instance variables always start with a lowercase letter. *See also* VARIABLE, POOL VARIABLE, CLASS VARIABLE, and GLOBAL VARIABLE.

ITERATIVE DESIGN and DEVELOPMENT. An approach to developing software that recognizes and takes advantage of our incomplete knowledge of the ProblemWorld. The idea is to make something work and then iteratively refine it until it is good enough to use. The only major problem is deciding when you're done. Works very well for dynamic, object-oriented development environments such as Smalltalk. *See also* PROBLEMWORLD, METHODOLOGY, and SOLUTIONWORLD.

JIM. A RealWorld human who needs to learn about object-oriented stuff. He lives in Milwaukee and is, indeed, a software developer.

KEYWORD MESSAGE. A message with one or more arguments. Made up of keywords, which begin with a letter and end with a colon. There is one keyword for each argument. *See also* MESSAGE and ORDER OF EXECUTION.

LATE BINDING. *See* DYNAMIC BINDING.

LOCAL VARIABLE. A variable available only during a single method activation. Defined within the source code for a method. Sometimes called temporary variables. *See also* VARIABLE and METHOD ACTIVATION.

MESSAGE. Something that is sent to an object to invoke a behavior, when that behavior is defined in a method. *See also* MESSAGE SELECTOR, UNARY MESSAGE, BINARY MESSAGE, KEYWORD MESSAGE, and METHOD.

MESSAGE INTERFACE. The set of nonprivate messages to which an object responds. *See also* PRIVATE METHODS.

METAPHOR. A thinking tool useful in object-oriented thinking and design. A concept transferred from its traditional framework to another, where it is used as an analogy or for implicit comparison. *See also* OBJECT-ORIENTED THINKING and ANALOGY.

METHOD. A piece of code executed when an object receives a message. *See also* MESSAGE and METHOD ACTIVATION.

METHOD ACTIVATION. When a message is sent to an object, it activates a method, creating any local variables, passing the arguments to the method's parameters, making `self` refer to the receiver object, and executing the method code. *See also* METHOD and MESSAGE.

METHODOLOGY. A system or method, usually including a sequential process that helps someone move from the ProblemWorld to the SolutionWorld. There is considerable commercial and research activity centered around the creation and standardization of a design and/or development methodology for object-oriented systems. So far everything available has holes big enough to chuck a horse through, but things are getting better.

OBJECT. What this is all about. Used as a focus for creating computer applications and can be used similarly in design and general thinking. Assumed to have two things, some information it keeps inside and some behavior or actions that can be activated from its outside.

OBJECT-ORIENTED DESIGN. A prolonged object-oriented thinking activity applied to a specific problem and solution. May be assisted by the use of a methodology. *See also* OBJECT-ORIENTED THINKING and METHOD-OLOGY.

OBJECT-ORIENTED PROGRAMMING. Programming using objects and messages. Doesn't really work unless you use a programming language designed with constructs supporting objects and messages. Also, the use of the concepts of class, inheritance, encapsulation, and polymorphism.

OBJECT-ORIENTED THINKING. Thinking about a problem or solution in terms of objects and messages. Also, the use of the concepts of class, inheritance, and polymorphism. *See also* OBJECT-ORIENTED DESIGN.

OBJECTIVE WIZARD. A virtual entity that knows a lot about object-oriented things, particularly those connected with Smalltalk. The knowledge and personality are based on several RealWorld people. *See also* WIZ.

OBJECTLAND. A virtual reality lurking inside dynamic, object-oriented systems such as Smalltalk. Where most of this book takes place.

OOD. Object-Oriented Design.

OOP. Object-Oriented Programming.

OOT. Object-Oriented Thinking.

ORDER OF EXECUTION. The order in which messages are sent and operations performed within a Smalltalk statement. The order (first to last): code in parentheses, unary messages, binary messages, keyword messages, assignment, and return. Multiple messages of the same type evaluate from left to right. *See also* UNARY MESSAGE, BINARY MESSAGE, and KEYWORD MESSAGE.

OVERRIDING. Methods inherited from a superclass can be overridden by writing another method with the same name in the subclass. The new method then is used. Only methods can be overridden. *See also* SUPER and INHERITANCE.

PANE. A section of a window controlled by an instance of a subclass of `SubPane`. Designed to interact with the user in a particular way. A set of classes implements different interaction strategies, such as text manipulation, list handling, and graphics. *See also* WINDOW.

PERSPECTIVE. A thinking tool useful in object-oriented thinking and design. The purposeful changing of the way an object is thought of or viewed. *See also* OBJECT-ORIENTED THINKING.

POLYMORPHISM. The ability of an object to decide how it will behave when it receives a message. In other words, the same message can invoke different behavior from different objects. In Smalltalk the behavior is defined by a method, and polymorphism is implemented using dynamic binding. In some object-oriented systems other than Smalltalk, polymorphism is built into the inheritance system, limiting its scope. *See also* DYNAMIC BINDING.

POOL DICTIONARY. A collection of pool variables stored in an instance of `Dictionary` and referenced by a global variable. Generally used to store collections of related constants, as in `CharacterConstants`. To use a pool dictionary, simply specify it in a class definition; it is then accessible to all the class and instance methods for that class. *See also* POOL VARIABLE.

POOL VARIABLE. A variable that can be shared between classes. Grouped into pool dictionaries, with the entire dictionary specified in the class definition. Treat pool variables, which always begin with a capital letter, in the same way as constants. Do not try to use an assignment on them. *See also* POOL DICTIONARY.

PROBLEMWORLD. The domain of a problem that needs to be solved. *See also* SOLUTIONWORLD and REALWORLD.

PRIVATE METHODS. Methods that are marked as private in their comment and are intended to be sent only from other methods in the same object. Private messages, which activate private methods, are not considered part of an object's message interface. This is a design distinction and is not enforced by the system. *See also* SELF and SUPER.

PSEUDO VARIABLE. An object that works like a variable but is not a variable. The Smalltalk language contains five pseudo variables: `true`, `false`, `nil`, `self`, and `super`. The first three are used to access an instance of the classes

`True`, `False`, and `UndefinedObject`, respectively. The second two are used to reference the receiver object. *See also* `SELF` and `SUPER`.

REALWORLD. Where we live. Sometimes called reality or real life. *See also* OBJECTLAND, COMPUTERLAND, PROBLEMWORLD, and SOLUTIONWORLD.

RECEIVER OBJECT. When talking about a message send, it is the object that receives the message. Within a method activation, it is the object that receives the message that activated that method. *See also* SELF and METHOD ACTIVATION.

RETURN. Every message send returns an object. To control what is returned you must use a return operation in the method code. The return character ($\wedge$) should be placed before the statement that returns the object you wish to return from your method. Also causes an exit from the method. Sometimes called answering an object.

SELF. The pseudo variable `self` refers to the receiver object. Most commonly used to send messages—often private messages—to the receiver object. *See also* PSEUDO VARIABLE, PRIVATE METHODS, RECEIVER OBJECT, and SUPER.

SENDER OBJECT. When talking about a message send, it is the object whose method activation is sending the message. This is confusing until you realize that all executing code in Smalltalk is happening within some object. *See also* RECEIVER OBJECT and METHOD ACTIVATION.

SENDERS. The methods that send a particular message, as in "the senders of the `size` message." Also, the option on the methods menu in the class hierarchy browser that creates a list of the senders of a message. *See also* IMPLEMENTORS.

SHOW IT. A menu option that compiles, executes, and displays the returned object from selected code in a text pane. Also, the action of selecting a piece of code and executing it with this menu option. *See also* DO IT.

SOLUTIONWORLD. The domain of the solution to a problem. There is often a large overlap between the ProblemWorld and the SolutionWorld. *See also* PROBLEMWORLD and REALWORLD.

STATEMENT. A chunk of Smalltalk code consisting of zero or more message sends and terminated by a period. Also called expression.

SUBCLASS. Denotes an inheritance relationship between two classes, as in "`Array` is a subclass of `Collection`." A subclass inherits from its superclass. *See also* SUPERCLASS and INHERITANCE.

SUPER. The pseudo variable `super` refers to the receiver object, but it behaves differently when sent a message. Messages sent to `super` start their search for the associated method in the object's superclass. Used only to access methods that have been overridden. *See also* **SELF,** SUPERCLASS, and OVERRIDING INHERITANCE.

SUPERCLASS. Denotes an inheritance relationship between two classes, as in "`Number` is the superclass of `Integer`." A subclass inherits from its superclass. *See also* SUBCLASS and INHERITANCE.

TEMPORARY VARIABLE. *See* LOCAL VARIABLE.

UNARY MESSAGE. A message with no arguments. Unary messages always begin with a lowercase letter. *See also* MESSAGE and ORDER OF EXECUTION.

VARIABLE. A sequence of characters beginning with a letter. When used in source code, it refers to some object. Does not have to refer to any particular object, just to some object. You can change the object that a variable references by using an assignment statement. Variables come in several flavors, which differ in where they can be used. *See also* ASSIGNMENT, INSTANCE VARIABLE, CLASS VARIABLE, LOCAL VARIABLE, and GLOBAL VARIABLE.

VISUALIZATION. A thinking tool useful in object-oriented thinking and design. The imaginary conceptualization of an object's attributes or state. Often combined with the animation of the object's behavior. *See also* OBJECT-ORIENTED THINKING and ANIMATION.

WINDOW. A construct that exists on a computer screen. Generally contains one or more subparts, called panes. This "screen thing" is used to do some particular task, such as writing words, editing method code, doing arithmetic, etc. *See also* PANE.

WIZ. Nickname for the Objective Wizard, used only by those who know him well.

WORKSPACE. A window in the Smalltalk programming environment. Used to type in brief pieces of temporary code. Often used for testing, trying out simple code, or keeping track of various odds and ends. A very simple and useful programming tool. *See also* WINDOW and APPLICATION.

REFERENCES

The following reference list is an excerpt from the ObjectLand library. I hope it will lead you in the right direction.

ObjectiveWizard

General Sources of Information

OOPSLA Conference Proceedings
ECOOPS Conference Proceedings

Journal of Object Oriented Programming (JOOP)
Object Magazine
The Smalltalk Report

Supporting References

Budd, T. A. 1991. *A Little Smalltalk.* Redding, Mass.: Addison-Wesley.

Cox, B. 1991. *Object-Oriented Programming: An Evolutionary Approach.* Redding, Mass.: Addison-Wesley.

Digitalk. 1992. *Smalltalk/V Windows Tutorial and Programming Handbook.* Los Angeles: Digitalk.

———. 1991. *Smalltalk /V DOSTutorial and Programming Handbook.* Los Angeles: Digitalk.

———. 1989. *Smalltalk /VPM Tutorial and Programming Handbook.* Los Angeles: Digitalk.

————. 1988. *Smalltalk /V286 Tutorial and Programming Handbook.* Los Angeles: Digitalk.

————. 1988. *Smalltalk /VMac Tutorial and Programming Handbook.* Los Angeles: Digitalk.

Entsminger, G. 1990. *The Toa of Objects.* Redwood City, La.: M&T Books.

Goldberg, A. and Robson, D. 1983. *Smalltalk-80: The Language and Its Implementation.* Redding, Mass.: Addison-Wesley.

Ingalls, D. 1980. *The Smalltalk-80 System Design and Implementation.* Palo Alto Xerox, Palo Alto Research Center.

————. The evolution of the Smalltalk virtual machine. In *Smalltalk-80: Bits of History, Words of Advice,* edited by Glen Krasner. Redding, Mass.: Addison-Wesley.

Pinson, J. L., and Wiener, R. S. 1988. *An Introduction to Object-Oriented Programming and Smalltalk.* Redding, Mass.: Addison-Wesley.

Savic, D. 1990. *Object-Oriented Programming with Smalltalk/V.* Englewood Cliffs, N.J.: Prentice Hall.

Shafer, D. 1991. *Practical Smalltalk: Using Smalltalk/V.* New York: Springer-Verlag.

Smith, David, N. 1991. *Concepts of Object-Oriented Programming.* New York: McGraw-Hill.

Taylor, D. 1992. *Object-Oriented Information Systems: Planning & Implementation.* New York: Wiley.

————. 1991. *Object-Oriented Technology: A Manager's Guide.* Redding, Mass.: Addison-Wesley.

INDEX